What people are saying abou

FORENSIC FaITH FOR KIDS

"An intriguing and compelling mystery that will capture the imagination of teens while delivering a much-needed message for youth and their parents today: you need to know what and why you believe in Jesus Christ. This novel will give parents some fresh opportunities to discuss matters of faith and convictions with their tweens and teens."

Dennis and Barbara Rainey, host of *FamilyLife Today* and cofounders of FamilyLife

"Detective Jim Wallace and his wife, Susie, have done it again—a story that is both important and fun! In trying to find the true owner of an adorable missing puppy, a group of young detectives discover truths about Jesus that will impact them (and you) forever. If you're a young person, you won't be able to put this one down."

Frank and Stephanie Turek, Christian apologist and founders of CrossExamined.org

"As parents, and perhaps even grandparents, there is little more important in this life than helping to 'shore up the faith' of our loved ones. *Forensic Faith for Kids* makes this task both easy and enjoyable. The book is not only very readable and entertaining for all generations, but most importantly, it is filled from cover to cover with apologetic truth. Whether an older saint or someone new to the faith, this book will prove itself invaluable."

Jeff and Dawn Siemon, Pro Bowl
Minnesota Vikings football player and
colaborers at Search Ministries

"J. Warner and Susie Wallace have brilliantly woven together a delightful mystery about a lost puppy with an everyday situation where the claims of Christ are challenged by a peer and shown how investigative techniques are critical in both of these dilemmas. *Forensic Faith for Kids* is chock full of tools to equip and encourage readers to be calm, confident investigators and communicators of our faith in Christ, and to trust that often the answers are hidden right in front of us … we just need to dig a little. A priceless book for kids of all ages!"

Jana and Ron Alayra, children's worship
leader, songwriter (including "Jump into the
Light"), producer, and recording artist

FORENSIC FAITH
FOR KIDS

FORENSIC FAITH

FOR KIDS

LEARN TO SHARE THE TRUTH FROM A REAL DETECTIVE

J. WARNER WALLACE AND SUSIE WALLACE
WITH ROB SUGGS

DAVID C COOK

transforming lives together

FORENSIC FAITH FOR KIDS
Published by David C Cook
4050 Lee Vance Drive
Colorado Springs, CO 80918 U.S.A.

Integrity Music Limited, a Division of David C Cook
Eastbourne, East Sussex BN23 6NT, England

The graphic circle C logo is a registered trademark of David C Cook.

The website addresses recommended throughout this book are offered as a
resource to you. These websites are not intended in any way to be or imply an
endorsement on the part of David C Cook, nor do we vouch for their content.

LCCN 2018934817
ISBN 978-0-7814-1458-6
eISBN 978-0-8307-7548-4

© 2018 James Warner Wallace
Published in association with the literary agency of Mark
Sweeney & Associates, Bonita Springs, FL 34135.

Illustrations by J. Warner Wallace
The Team: Stephanie Bennett, Amy Konyndyk, Jack Campbell, Susan Murdock
Cover Design and Illustration: Nick Lee

Printed in the United States of America
First Edition 2018

1 2 3 4 5 6 7 8 9 10

062918

CONTENTS

BEFORE YOU BEGIN

My name is J. Warner Wallace and I'm a "cold-case" detective. That means I solve difficult cases that have been unsolved for a long time. I wanted to be a detective when I was very young, and I worked hard to achieve my goals, first by accepting my duty as a police officer, and then by training and advancing to the level of detective. Along the way I learned how to investigate mysteries and share the truths I discovered with others.

When I was first assigned to the detective division at my police agency, Alan Jeffries was the most experienced detective in the unit. He was tough and a bit "rough around the edges," but the more I got to know him, the more I came to understand that he cared deeply about my progress as a new detective. He had a "soft side" that he showed on occasion, and I began to look *forward* to my conversations with him. He became my mentor and reminded me of my duty as he trained me to investigate and share the truth.

Years after meeting Alan Jeffries, I applied everything I learned as a detective to my investigation of the Bible. I wanted to know if the Bible was telling me the truth about Jesus, and after several months, I determined that Jesus truly *is* the Son of God. That's why

I'm a Christian today, and it's also why I want to share the truth with everyone I know.

Now it's time for you to learn how to be a good detective, and Alan Jeffries will help you achieve that goal.

If you like to solve mysteries, you're in the right place. My wife, Susie, and I have written two other books, *Cold-Case Christianity for Kids* and *God's Crime Scene for Kids*, that describe mysteries involving a skateboard and a shoebox. This time around, the Junior Detective Cadets are investigating something even *more* interesting: the sudden appearance of a *puppy*! Are you ready to accept your duty as a detective cadet, train with Detective Jeffries, and learn how to investigate and share the case? If so, turn the page and jump into the story.

And by the way, be sure to invite your family to join you. Your parents, grandparents, or older siblings can follow along with you and even read the adult version of this book, *Forensic Faith*, and everyone can go online to the Case Makers Academy at www.ForensicFaithforKids.com to watch videos, download fun activity sheets, and even earn a graduation certificate when you're all done.

Well … what are you waiting for? Turn the page and join the investigation!

J. Warner Wallace

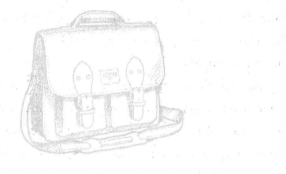

"Stop whining..." says Daniel as he throws you a fresh towel.

A New Challenge

Where Did She Come From?

"I'm getting a cramp in my shoulder," complains Jason as he wipes water off the hood of the fourteenth car in a row.

"Stop whining," says Daniel while throwing you a fresh towel. "We've all been working just as hard as you have." Daniel smiles in your direction and rolls his eyes.

"We're almost done," you say. "And remember, it's for a good cause." You point to a large handmade banner at the entry to the recreation center parking lot: BASEBALL TEAM CAR WASH TODAY.

Daniel tugs at his uniform shirt and points to Jason's. "You wanna play, right? We've got to raise money to go to the tournament one way or another. This is as good as any."

Jason looks as though he agrees and keeps drying the hood.

It's late in the afternoon on a warm spring Sunday, and there are wet, soapy cars across the entire parking lot. All your teammates are busy washing or drying, and everyone seems to be as tired as Jason. The three of you arrived right after church and helped turn the rec center parking lot into a makeshift car wash with hoses, buckets, and *lots* of towels. The sun is beginning to set, but there are still a few more customers.

Daniel reaches for another towel when he feels something *licking* his leg. He looks down toward the pavement and sees a small puppy standing next to his leg and … *smiling* at him.

"Whoa, check this out!" Daniel bends down to pet the tiny dog, but before he can do so, the puppy rolls over on its back and invites a belly rub. You and Jason laugh.

The puppy rolls over on its back and invites a belly rub.

"Pembroke Welsh corgi!" exclaims Jason.

"What language are you speaking?" asks Daniel.

"Dog language. I mean, not dog language, but that's what kind of dog it is. My uncle is a veterinarian, and he has a poster in his

waiting room showing all the breeds of
dog. This is a corgi all right."

CSI Assignment

The group is trying to decide what to do with the puppy. Read Psalm 25:2.

In times of uncertainty, King David said he would choose to trust _____.

The little puppy has oversized ears,
short legs, and a stub for a tail. Her fur is
soft and tan and white in color.

"Where did she come from?" you ask.

"I don't know," replies Daniel. "I didn't
see any of our customers with a dog, and
I know none of our teammates brought
theirs ..."

"Well, she must belong to someone,"
says Jason. "She's got a collar." Jason carefully turns the woven band and finds a name printed on the top:
BAILEY.

"I guess her name is Bailey then," you say.

Daniel picks up the puppy and the three of you begin to search for
her owner. The last few cars are almost finished, and many of the team
parents are starting to clean up and collect the buckets and towels.

"Does anyone here own this puppy?!" shouts Jason. No one
responds.

The other baseball team members and their parents now gather
around Daniel as he cradles little Bailey. The puppy is incredibly
friendly and continues to lick Daniel's face as he holds her. Your
teammates are entranced by the little pup, but no one has any idea
where she came from.

"This is so strange," declares Daniel. "Where *did* she come from?
How could such a small puppy like this appear out of *thin air*? And
why is she so incredibly *friendly*?"

Jason steps through the small crowd of baseball players. "Let's take her back to your house and see what your parents think we should do." The three of you say good-bye to your team and begin to walk to Daniel's house.

"Maybe my parents will let me keep her," says Daniel.

"I don't know," you reply. "She does have a collar, after all. I bet her owners are worried about her."

Back at Daniel's house, his parents agree with you.

"No, I don't think we can keep her, Son …" says Daniel's dad as he sits in a comfortable chair in the living room. "But I can certainly see why you like her." Bailey is climbing all over Daniel's father's lap and licking his neck and face. The puppy's little stub of a tail is wagging back and forth at incredible speed. "She's the friendliest dog I've ever seen."

Daniel's mom enters the room carrying a tray of cookies. "Don't you have another Junior Detective Academy session tomorrow at the police department? Why don't we keep her overnight and tomorrow you can take Bailey with you to the Academy. Maybe Detective Jeffries can help you figure out where Bailey came from and what you should do with her. He's used to solving mysteries, right?"

Jason is already eating his second cookie. "He's the best, and I bet he'll be happy to see we've got another mystery to investigate."

Dig Deep
Visit the Online Academy

Be sure to complete the Training Activities and Note Sheets.
    Start assembling your Academy Notebook!

"Yup," you reply. "Only this time we're not trying to solve a mystery about a '*what*'—this time we're trying to solve a mystery about a '*who*!'"

Chapter One

BAILEY

What Is "Faith" Anyway?

Duty Begins with a Definition

Hannah walks into the Sunday night meeting of her church's youth group. She's glad to be there, but she's lost in her thoughts. Just prior to leaving her house, Daniel called to say he had a new mystery to offer at tomorrow's Junior Detective Academy session, but he wouldn't tell her *anything* about it. Hannah and Daniel have investigated mysteries together at two different junior academies, but this time Daniel wants their next mystery to remain ... *a mystery*! Now it's almost all Hannah can think about.

As the worship music begins, Hannah smiles at her friends as she settles in and focuses on the words of each song. Just before the singing ends, Hannah's friend Tiana sits down next to her. Tiana sings a few words from the last song but seems preoccupied and looks over her shoulder several times.

When the music ends, Hannah turns to Tiana. "Hi, Tiana, who's that boy you're looking at?" she asks as she nods across the large room to the tall slender boy standing way off by the entryway. "I can see you're distracted by him."

She nods across the large room to the tall slender boy standing way off by the entryway.

"His name is Marco ..." replies Tiana. Hannah smiles, and waits for more. "What?" says Tiana, responding to Hannah's curious smile. "He's just a friend from school." Hannah smiles even more broadly. "No, seriously, Hannah, I just go to school with him ... but I will admit that I've been worried about him lately."

From a distance, Hannah can see that Marco has his hands in his pockets and seems uncomfortable, and even a bit *sad*.

"I've never seen him at church before," mentions Hannah as she begins to walk toward Marco to try to cheer him up and invite him into the group.

Tiana pulls Hannah aside. "You're right, he's never been to our church. That's one of the reasons why I've been thinking about him," she says. "I invited Marco to youth group a week ago, but he told me that he thought it was a *waste of time*. He said that he's not sure if God exists, but he's *certain* that Jesus is *not* God."

"He said that he's not sure if God exists, but he's certain that Jesus is not God."

Hannah pauses to hear more.

"He reads a lot, and he says he's even read all the Gospels to learn what they teach about Jesus ..." Tiana lowers her voice and leans closer to Hannah. "He said that he thinks Jesus was just a smart man. Nothing more. In fact, he said that after reading the Gospels, he couldn't find a single place where Jesus ever said, 'I am God.'" Tiana looks genuinely concerned.

Hannah just smiles.

"Doesn't that bug you, Hannah?" asks Tiana with a quizzical expression on her face. "Why are you smiling? If Jesus didn't think He was God, why should Marco? Why should *we* think Jesus is God if *He* didn't say He was God?"

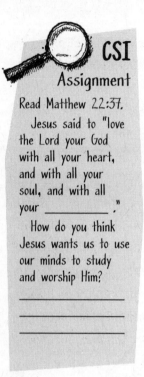

CSI Assignment

Read Matthew 22:37.

Jesus said to "love the Lord your God with all your heart, and with all your soul, and with all your _____."

How do you think Jesus wants us to use our minds to study and worship Him?

_____

_____

_____

Hannah takes a deep breath. "I wish you would have joined the detective cadet academy with me and Daniel. We've already investigated Jesus and found there is good evidence to believe He *rose from the grave.*"

Tiana looks a bit surprised. "You *investigated* Jesus? You mean like a detective? I didn't even know you could do that."

"Why not?" asks Hannah. "God created us with brains, right? I think He wants us to use them."

"But I thought 'having faith' means believing in something *without* any evidence," says Tiana. "My parents even said that when I told them about Marco."

Hannah considers Tiana's words for a moment and realizes that tears are starting to form in Tiana's eyes. "Hannah, I've been a Christian for as long as I can remember. My parents are Christians. But what if Marco's right? What if Jesus was just another smart man?"

"Are you starting to doubt Christianity is true, Tiana?" asks Hannah.

"I guess I am …" answers Tiana reluctantly. "I just don't know what to say to Marco."

"Let's just begin by saying hello," says Hannah. "We've been kinda rude to let him stand there by himself all this time." She begins to walk in Marco's direction. "Why does he look so sad, by the way?" she asks.

"He told me that he's worried about his mom," replies Tiana. "Marco's mom has been upset all day, but she wouldn't tell him what's wrong ..."

Hannah approaches Marco a step ahead of Tiana. "Hi, Marco, I'm Hannah, glad you could join us tonight." She and Tiana escort Marco to the rows of seating where they find a spot and get ready to listen to the youth pastor.

The next day, a beautiful Monday afternoon, Daniel is amazed at Bailey's energy and speed as he walks her to the police department. He's doing his best to control her with the makeshift leash his dad made from some rope in the garage, but she's a handful. How can such a *small* puppy, with such *short, stubby* legs, run so *fast*?

As Daniel approaches the station, he sees you, Jason, Hannah, and several other cadets arriving for the next Junior Detective Academy session. As soon as Hannah sees Bailey, she begins to run toward Daniel and the puppy.

"Is *this* the mystery you were talking about last night?" she asks excitedly.

Daniel grins. "Yup. Pretty amazing, right?"

"Yeah, but I don't get it," she replies. "What's the mystery?"

Detective Definitions

K-9 Units:

Police officers who are paired with specially trained dogs.

The expression "K-9" is coined from the word "canine," the scientific term used for dogs. Police dogs are used to search for drugs or explosives, to locate missing people, and to find crime scene evidence.

"You'll see ..." you say, as everyone files into the lobby of the police department.

"Hang on a minute there!" shouts Service Officer Margolin as soon as he sees the puppy enter the building. "Unless that's a K-9 dog, you can't bring it in the station."

Just then, Detective Alan Jeffries storms into the lobby from the Detective Division. He looks even more stern than usual when he first sees Daniel holding something at the end of a leash. "Yes, you cadets know better than that," he says in his *serious* voice. "We have rules here, and—" He stops abruptly when he sees Bailey. "Uh. Who is this?"

Detective Jeffries's facial expression softens immediately as he bends down to pet the puppy. You've seen this expression before when Jeffries met Jason's cat, Simba. Bailey is smiling again as the detective stoops down to pet her.

"Wow, this might be the cutest dog I've ever seen," remarks Detective Jeffries as Bailey immediately rolls on her back for another belly rub.

"And the friendliest too," adds Jason.

Daniel quickly offers an explanation. "She just showed up out of nowhere while we were working at a car wash fundraiser yesterday at the rec center. No one has any idea where she came from, so we thought we would bring her here to see if you could help us solve the mystery."

Detective Jeffries looks at Daniel with a bit of skepticism. "So, you thought you could cleverly persuade me to investigate another mystery if it involved this adorable puppy?" he asks with a serious look on his face. Daniel doesn't know what to say, and everyone else remains quiet to see what Jeffries will do. "Well, it worked," replies Detective Jeffries, answering his own question. The cadets laugh as he directs everyone toward the briefing room.

"Officer Margolin, can you radio Animal Control Officer Bargar and have him join us?" asks Detective Jeffries as he picks up the puppy and cradles her. As they walk toward the briefing room, Jeffries talks gently to Bailey in a voice usually reserved for small children or babies.

Jeffries talks gently to Bailey in a voice usually reserved for small children or babies.

"Can you believe how he's cuddling Bailey?" whispers Hannah.

"I heard that!" barks Jeffries. "Remember, I have detective ears. Don't let this moment fool you. I'm still a tough guy!"

Everyone laughs.

Once you're all assembled in the briefing room, Detective Jeffries hands Bailey to Jason and writes a word on the whiteboard: DUTY.

"All of us, as citizens, have a duty to determine the truth about who might own a dog or cat we discover is lost in our community. Agreed?"

All the cadets nod their heads. Detective Jeffries continues, "Daniel, I bet when you first found Bailey, you felt like keeping her ..."

"She *is* a cute dog ..." admits Daniel.

"But you brought her here anyway," adds Jeffries, "in *spite* of how you felt. In other words, you knew you had a duty to do more than simply follow your feelings."

Detective Jeffries stops as everyone hears a knock on the briefing room door. Animal Control Officer Bargar enters the room. Unlike the other police officers who wear navy-blue uniforms, Officer Bargar is wearing a tan-and-brown uniform. He doesn't carry a gun, but instead has a plain leather belt with a radio holster.

"Cadets, this is Officer Bargar," announces Detective Jeffries. "He'll take a report and find Bailey's owner."

Daniel suddenly realizes that Officer Bargar is trained to return dogs like Bailey

CSI Assignment

It's not always wise to trust your feelings alone.

Read Proverbs 28:26.

"He who trusts in his own _____ is a fool, but he who walks _____ will be delivered."

Why do you think it's better to trust knowledge and wisdom than it is to trust your heart and feelings?

_____

_____

to their owners. Daniel seems to understand that he is about to hand Bailey over, and he is visibly disappointed. Everyone can tell that he's sad to be separated from the puppy, and Officer Bargar can see it too.

"Daniel, can I ask you a favor?" Officer Bargar asks as he begins to take a report. "After I'm done with this report, can you take the dog home with you until we find her owner? Our kennels are full right now, and it would sure help us with the overcrowding."

"Daniel, can I ask you a favor?"

Daniel perks up and smiles. You wonder if Officer Bargar is just trying to be nice, but you are happy for Daniel anyway.

"Sure!" says Daniel.

"I have an idea," says Detective Jeffries. "If it's okay with you, Officer Bargar, can *we* investigate this case to figure out where Bailey belongs? It might be the perfect way to start a new academy: a *Forensic Investigations Academy*. Does that sound all right to you?"

"Sounds great," says Officer Bargar, and then he begins to ask Daniel questions for the report.

"Can my neighbor Jasmine join us for this investigation?" asks Jason. "Ever since we investigated the shoebox in my attic, she's been asking to join us."

"Of course," says Detective Jeffries. "Have her fill out an application before the next meeting."

 Officer Bargar finishes up his report as the meeting begins to wind down. Hannah asks a question: "Detective Jeffries, can I add to the caseload? We're good at working on more than one mystery at a time, I've noticed."

"Tell us what you've got."

Hannah shares her experience with Tiana and Marco, both of whom have some big questions about Jesus. "I know Jesus is the Son of God," says Hannah. "The prior academy helped me investigate that. But Marco told Tiana that he read all the Gospels and didn't find a single place where Jesus said, 'I am God.'" The cadets are paying close attention now, and you are thinking about everything you learned about Jesus at the prior Junior Detective Academy.

"At first, it didn't really bother me, but then I went home and started to think about it. I'm also like Tiana—I've been a Christian since I was a little kid, and maybe I've taken it for granted."

Detective Definitions

Duty:

The actions or tasks required by a person's position or occupation.

Police officers, for example, must perform certain duties as part of their job.

Christians also have a duty to live as Jesus would have us live and be ready to give the reason for our hope in Him.

"Lots of Christians have a similar story," says Detective Jeffries as he pulls a chair up to the table and sits down.

"I tried to find a place in the Gospels where Jesus said, 'I am God,'" explains Hannah. "I got frustrated pretty quickly. The Gospels are long and sometimes hard to understand. I skimmed through a couple of them but I couldn't find Jesus saying, 'I am God.'" Hannah pauses. "It's bugging me. Tiana said something I can't forget. She said, 'If Jesus didn't think He was God, why should Marco? Why should *anyone* think Jesus is God if *He* didn't say He was God?'"

After hearing this, you also wonder how you might respond to someone like Tiana or Marco.

"I'm so glad that we are talking about duty today," says Detective Jeffries as he looks at Hannah directly, then at the rest of the cadets. "It's an important topic as we begin the Forensic Investigations Academy."

Jeffries stands up and returns to the whiteboard. "Citizens have duties, and so do Christians. One of the most important duties we

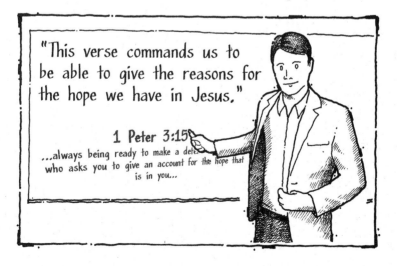

"This verse commands us to be able to give the reasons for the hope we have in Jesus."

1 Peter 3:15
...always being ready to make a defe who asks you to give an account for the hope that is in you...

have as Christians is to be able to answer tough questions like the one asked by Marco and Tiana." Jeffries writes a verse on the board: 1 Peter 3:15. "This verse commands us to be able to give the *reasons* for the hope we have in Jesus. God wouldn't ask us to do this if there *weren't* any good reasons to believe."

Detective Jeffries points toward Daniel. "Just like Daniel when he was trying to decide what to do with Bailey; we can't simply follow our feelings. Daniel had to remember his duty related to Bailey, and we have to remember our duty related to Jesus. We need to have good reasons that we can share with others."

"I agree," says Hannah, "but Tiana said something else interesting. She said she thought 'having faith' meant believing in something *without* any evidence."

"Ahh ... the word 'faith,'" says Detective Jeffries as he draws three columns on the whiteboard. In the first one, he writes "Unreasonable Faith"; in the second, "Blind Faith"; and in the third, "Forensic Faith." "Let's consider three possible ways to talk about 'faith.'"

UNREASONABLE FAITH	BLIND FAITH	FORENSIC FAITH
"in spite of" the evidence	"without" any evidence	"because of" the evidence

Jeffries points to the first definition. "You could put your faith in something *in spite of* evidence that shows it's untrue. Like believing that you can get warts from frogs. People used to believe that, but now we have good evidence that shows we *don't* get warts from frogs."

"So, that would be an *unreasonable* belief," you say.

"That's right, but our belief that *Christianity* is true isn't *unreasonable*, because we've got good evidence to *show* that it's true."

"Like the evidence we investigated in the other Academy," says Jason.

"Exactly," replies Detective Jeffries as he now points to the second column. "We could also have faith that something is true *without any evidence at all.*"

"But then how would we know for sure if it's true?" you ask.

Jeffries smiles. "That's a great question. If you trust something is true *without any evidence*, you could be right, or you could be wrong. You would never know for sure, though, because you're not relying on any evidence."

Hannah speaks up. "Is that what Tiana was talking about when she said she thought 'having faith' meant believing in something *without* any evidence?"

Detective Definitions

Forensic:

The adjective "forensic" comes from the Latin word *forensis*, which means "in open court" or "public."

Detectives use evidence in public courts to make their case, and Christians can use evidence to make their case publicly as well.

"Probably," replies Jeffries, "but that's not what Jesus expected from His followers. He always provided them with evidence, including His ability to *rise from the grave*, to show that He was telling the truth."

Detective Jeffries now moves over to the third column. "When you put your faith in something *because of the evidence*, you have what I call a 'forensic faith': a faith that can be shared *publicly* because it's based on good evidence."

"But wait a minute," blurts out Jason. "If you're using evidence to show that something is true, why are you calling it 'faith' at all?"

"If you're using evidence to show that something is true, why are you calling it 'faith' at all?"

"That's an even better question, Jason. I can tell you're thinking hard about these definitions."

Jason looks like he's glad he asked a good question.

"Even though you might use evidence to figure out if something is true, you're still going to have some questions that are difficult, if not impossible, to answer. In every case I've investigated and presented to a jury, there were some questions I just couldn't answer for the jurors. Even *great cases* built on *good evidence* have *unanswerable questions*. But we still ask jurors to make a decision, and they *do* make a decision, *in spite of* the fact they don't have all the evidence they might like."

Jeffries turns toward Jason. "Jurors make a decision based on evidence, even though they have some unanswered questions. That's what a good 'forensic faith' is all about."

Hannah still looks puzzled. "So, what should I tell Tiana?"

Jeffries puts down the whiteboard marker. "Remind her that having a forensic faith means you may still have a few unanswered questions, and that's okay. And then tell her that we're going to add her question about Jesus to our investigation in this Forensic Investigations Academy."

Detective Jeffries picks up the marker and starts writing assignments on the whiteboard. "Here are your 'marching orders' until the next time we meet: First, use your detective skills to find some evidence related to Bailey. I would start around the area where you first found her. Second, start to read through the Gospels and look for evidence that would prove Jesus is God. Be creative and ask for help from people who might know the Bible better than you do."

A "Tool" for Your Detective Bag!

Accept Your Duty

Being a Christian means accepting your duty as Peter described in 1 Peter 3:15. Recommit yourself as a Christian to learn about the evidence for Jesus and for God's existence. Become a Christian "case maker"!

Jeffries walks over to Bailey and picks up the puppy, as he thanks Officer Bargar for his help. "Let's learn how to be good detectives as we figure out who Bailey belongs to ... and who Jesus claimed to be."

As they leave the room, there's lots of excited chatter—and one happy bark.

Two nights later, Hannah and Tiana are talking on the phone.

Don't Be a Quitter
Duty Requires Determination

Two nights later, Hannah and Tiana are talking on the phone. "How are things with Marco?" asks Hannah.

"He still seems concerned about his mom. I guess she's still upset about something …"

"Did he say anything about youth group?" Hannah is eager to know.

"He said it was '*interesting*,' but he doesn't really want to come back. He says he has better things to do." Tiana's voice seems a bit shaky. "Lately I've been wondering if he's right. He seems so *certain* that Jesus was just a smart man and nothing more, you know?"

Hannah pauses, trying to think of exactly how she should respond.

Detective Definitions

Evidence:

Anything that shows a claim to be true (or false) can be offered as evidence.

Lots of different things could be used to show that Jesus is God, including things He said about Himself and miracles He worked to show that He had the power of God. His Resurrection would be the greatest piece of evidence—only God Himself would be able to raise Himself from the grave.

Tiana begins again before Hannah can say anything. "I did ask a few of my Christian friends to help me answer what Marco said about Jesus, but they weren't sure what to say either. If no one has an answer, maybe there *isn't* an answer."

This triggers Hannah's memory. "Tiana, even *great cases* built on *good evidence* have *unanswered questions*. I learned that this week from Detective Jeffries at the Academy."

Tiana is silent for a moment. Hannah takes a deep breath and continues, "Just because you and I may not know an answer *yet* doesn't mean there isn't an answer *at all*."

"I guess that makes sense," replies Tiana.

"I'm going to start an investigation this week on what Marco's been saying about Jesus. If you'll give me a few days, I'll get back to you. I'm a detective, after all!"

Tiana laughs.

After hanging up with Tiana, Hannah decides to return to her Bible to collect some evidence. She flips through the Scripture, trying to decide where to begin. A knock on her bedroom door breaks her concentration.

"Are you about ready for dinner?" asks her dad as he pokes his head in.

"Almost," says Hannah. "Do you have a second?"

"I've got an *hour* if you need it," says her dad as he sits on the end of her bed.

Hannah tells her father about Tiana and how she's been struggling with what Marco's been saying about Jesus. She even confesses her own concerns. "Dad, at first it really bothered me that I couldn't think of what to say to Tiana, but Detective Jeffries told me to start collecting evidence from my Bible. I'm just not sure where to begin …"

"Well, it sounds like Detective Jeffries wants you to read through the Bible and see if you can find places where Jesus said He was God. Is that right?"

"Yes, I think so," says Hannah, "but that's a *lot* of reading!"

"How about this?" replies Hannah's dad as he opens the Bible. "The shortest gospel in the Bible is the gospel of Mark. Why don't you read through it to see what you find?"

Hannah remembers reading through this gospel in one of her academies with Detective Jeffries. "Okay, that's a good idea. I'm already familiar with it."

"In the meantime, Mom and I have our Bible study tomorrow night and we'll ask our group to start looking for evidence as well. It may take awhile, but maybe we can help you build a case." He smiles and suddenly holds his stomach. Hannah hears a *rumble*. "Oh, I think my stomach is telling me it's time to eat!"

"Dad," teases Hannah, "you *always* think it's time to eat."

 Across town, you, Jason, and Jasmine are standing on Daniel's front porch, waiting for him to answer the doorbell. He opens the door and is glad to see all of you, but especially Jasmine.

"Hey, did you turn in your application?" he asks Jasmine.

Jasmine laughs. "Yes, I turned it in yesterday, and Detective Jeffries said it seems fine. You're looking at the newest cadet!"

Their conversation is interrupted by a joyful bark and a stub-wagging appearance from Bailey as she pushes her way between Daniel's legs and onto the front porch.

"Oh my, she really is as cute as you said, Jason," says Jasmine as she rubs Bailey's belly. "She's *enchanting*."

"I've never heard a dog called *that*," you say.

"She's a corgi, right? I watched a television program about these dogs. Did you know that there are really old legends and make-believe stories about these little dogs?"

"Really?" asks Daniel. He seems skeptical.

"Yup, the old fantasy stories described fairies and elves using corgis to pull their carriages, and they would even ride corgis like horses when battling with one another," says Jasmine calmly as she continues to rub the puppy's belly.

Daniel and Jason look at each other. Is this why Bailey showed up mysteriously "out of nowhere"? Does this explain why she is as fast as a horse?

"No wonder we couldn't find the owner," jokes Jason. "He's invisible!"

"Let's take a more reasonable approach," answers Daniel, a bit impatiently. "Detective Jeffries said we should start in the area where we first found Bailey. My mom said she'd be willing to go door to door with us to see if anyone in that neighborhood knows anything about Bailey."

CSI Assignment

Read John 14:11.

Jesus said, "Believe Me that I am in the Father and the Father is in Me; otherwise believe because of the _____ themselves."

What kind of evidence did Jesus ask people to look at?

_____

Everybody agrees it's a good idea, but hours later they return to Daniel's house without any new information. No one seems to know anything about a missing dog.

"Next idea," says Jason. "Let's make some 'missing pet' signs. The signs could do the asking for us, even while we're at school." So, with the help of Daniel's mom (and her computer), you create "Found Dog" signs, complete with Daniel's home phone number. Thirty minutes later, you and your friends have posted signs all over the neighborhood.

At the next session of the Forensic Investigations Academy, the cadets are a little frustrated and discouraged. Hannah read through the entire gospel of Mark and couldn't find anything helpful, and Daniel doesn't have any new information about Bailey. Everyone is assembled in the briefing room, waiting for the arrival of Detective Jeffries. Jasmine is wearing her new cadet uniform for the first time. No one is saying much, however, and even Bailey looks tired as she takes a nap on the floor next to Daniel.

Jasmine pipes up. "This is my first session with you guys, and everyone looks defeated. No one even said how great I look in this uniform!" Just then, Bailey lies flat on her stomach like she's Superman. Her front paws are stretched completely forward, and her rear legs are stretched out behind her. She's sleeping peacefully but looks like she's flying across the floor. Jasmine notices and starts to laugh. That gets everyone's attention.

"That's called a corgi 'sploot,'" informs Jason. Bailey's funny lounging position cheers everyone up for a moment as Detective Jeffries enters the room.

"That's called a corgi 'sploot,'" says Jason.

"That dog gets cuter by the moment," he says as Bailey continues to snooze. "Since you still have her, I'm guessing you haven't solved the mystery."

"Not even close," answers Daniel. "Do you think we should return her to Officer Bargar and let him work on the case?"

Detective Jeffries says, "You mean after weeks and months of investigation?"

"No!" says Daniel, confused. "It's just been a few days—"

"Exactly my point. You haven't even had time to get a good start and you're giving up?"

Detective Jeffries looks very serious as he speaks to the cadets from the front of the room. "Good detectives are stubborn—in a *good* way. We work a case until there are no angles left to pursue. We ask every question available to be asked. Right?"

The cadets all agree.

"You're a group of *detectives*. I've trained you myself! I expect you to be *thorough*. Now tell me what you've got so far."

"So far—*elves*," says Jason.

"So far - elves," says Jason.

Detective Jeffries raises an eyebrow. Some of the cadets laugh.

"He's talking about make-believe stories and legends," says Jasmine, explaining what she saw on television.

"Conclusions?" asks Jeffries.

Detective Definitions
Case Maker:

Case makers have to do two things: gather evidence and share it with others.

The Bible describes us as case makers. We must learn how to gather the evidence and share it with others so we will be "ready to make a defense" to anyone who wants to know why you think Christianity is true.

"I'll admit, I thought about how fast Bailey runs," says Daniel. "And the fact that she kind of appeared out of nowhere ..."

"So, that's evidence she's an 'enchanted dog'?"

The cadets look at each other a bit uncomfortably.

"I guess fantasy explanations aren't the same as evidence," Hannah says.

"I would agree," says Detective Jeffries. "Daniel's observations are that Bailey is fast, and that she seems to have come from nowhere; those are facts. Can we explain them apart from stories about elves and fairies? By the way, do we have any evidence that *fairies and elves exist in the first place*?"

Hannah says, "I guess we need forensic beliefs, not unreasonable or blind ones. So, we need better evidence."

"Exactly," says Jeffries, pleased that Hannah understands the difference.

 "And that brings me to your investigation. What did you find in your study of the Bible?"

"Not much, at least in terms of what Jesus *said* about Himself." Hannah pulls her Bible from her backpack. "I've only read the gospel of Mark so far, and I see lots of places where Jesus does things that only God would be able to do, but I still can't find a place where he says, 'I am God.' I'm pretty discouraged and I was wondering if you would be willing to talk with Tiana or Marco—I don't think I can actually help them."

"Whoa, wait a minute here," says Detective Jeffries as he picks up a whiteboard marker. "Those miracles you talked about in the gospel of Mark are part of the case for Jesus being God, so don't be so quick to discount them. And I bet you may have missed a few other forms of evidence that would help you make your case …"

Hannah is interested to hear more.

"But there's a bigger issue I'm hearing from all of you today. Daniel came here ready to hand Bailey's case back to Officer Bargar, and now you're ready to hand your case to *me*."

The cadets look a bit embarrassed as they realize they were close to giving up.

The detective says, "I think you can track down a little dog's owner, and I think you can learn to talk about your faith. Hannah, you have one thing I don't have: a friendship with Tiana and Marco. And friendship counts for a lot."

"I see what you mean. But it's a little scary."

"I know it seems that way. But you're not alone! You'll be part of a two-thousand-year-old line of men and women, boys and girls, who have studied the evidence for their faith and defended it before others."

Detective Jeffries turns to the board and writes the words "Case Makers" and underlines them. Under this, he starts to draw a picture of Jesus.

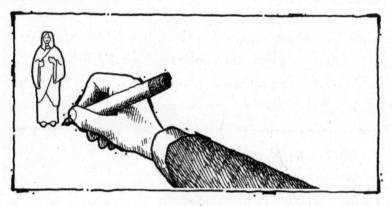

"Jesus didn't ask people to believe what He said about Himself without providing *evidence*," he says. "He often pointed people to witnesses or to His miracles as evidence to prove His statements."

Jeffries then draws a picture of several men standing together.

"After Jesus ascended into heaven, His disciples served as eyewitnesses. Do you remember what *that* form of evidence is called?"

"Yes, witnesses are 'direct evidence,'" answers Hannah.

"Correct," says Detective Jeffries. "One of the books in the New Testament is called the *Acts of the Apostles*, or simply the *Book of Acts*. Next time you read it, notice how the apostles share the truth about

Jesus—they always testify as eyewitnesses of the Resurrection. They continued to use direct evidence to make their case."

Next, Detective Jeffries draws a picture of a man writing on a scroll.

"Some of the disciples of Jesus wrote the books we now have in the New Testament. They were trusted to write these books because they were using direct evidence: the statements of the eyewitnesses who knew Jesus personally."

The next part of Jeffries's illustration is a group of men in ancient clothing.

"After the disciples died, many of the earliest Christians were 'case makers' who had to defend what they believed because they were living at a time when Christianity wasn't popular. These men were known for their ability to make the case."

Detective Jeffries finishes his drawing by adding a picture of a boy and a girl. He looks carefully back and forth at Jasmine and Jason as he completes the diagram.

"Hey, are you trying to draw *us*?" asks Jason.

"That depends," responds Jeffries. "Do you think it looks like you?"

"A little …" says Jason.

"Then, *yes*. It *is* a drawing of you!"

The cadets laugh.

"For the entire history of Christianity, regular people like you and me have been making the case for Jesus. We're commanded to do this, just like Peter said in his letter. It's our duty to find and study the evidence so we can make the case to others."

Jesus   The   The   The   Us
            Disciples   Authors   Ancients

Jasmine says, "It makes you wonder—what if people our age stopped doing that? What if none of us wanted to make the case?"

"It seems to me like God would always find somebody new to do it," replies Hannah.

"I think you're right," says Detective Jeffries. "And I think He's doing that right now. Which means we need to find the evidence, study it, and make the case—just as we're trying to do with Bailey and with Marco's claims about Jesus."

The cadets still seem perplexed about how to do this.

"I have a couple pointers for you," says Jeffries, sensing their concern. "Daniel, you started off well, even though it doesn't seem that way. You all did a good job trying to talk to everyone in the neighborhood. I want you to think about experts or witnesses you might like to interview. Try to find some physical evidence to examine.

"Hannah, you also started well. Now, I'm going to go home tonight and think about a strategy you might take to investigate

A "Tool" for Your

Detective Bag!

Take Your Place

You are called to be part of the long line of Christian case makers that Detective Jeffries described. That means you'll need to learn how to gather evidence and then share what you've found with others. Are you ready?

the Bible. Meanwhile, you do your best to continue to read through the other gospels to see what you can learn."

Jeffries then looks at all the cadets. "One more question for the group. What's the biggest lesson for today?"

Daniel wrinkles his brow and says, "I give up."

"Wrong! It's *don't* give up!"

Everybody leaves the briefing room laughing.

"I think we better solve this mystery soon before I get any more attached to this little puppy."

Time to Train!

Training Starts with a Frustrating Test

Daniel and Hannah take what Detective Jeffries said *seriously*. When Daniel meets you after school, he's already picked up Bailey from his house. He's eager and ready to go.

"I think we better solve this mystery soon before I get any more attached to this little puppy," he says as Bailey smiles her usual charming smile.

You and Daniel head over to Jason's house on your way to the next Academy meeting. "We might as well ask Jasmine to join us on the way to the station," you say. "Since she lives right next door to Jason."

Jason meets you on his porch and agrees. "I know Jasmine's home," he says. "I could hear her talking to someone over the back-yard fence."

The three of you knock on Jasmine's door and wait for an answer. A few minutes go by without a response. Eventually Jasmine's mom answers. "Hi, kids," she says as she looks at your cadet uniforms. "I bet you're here to pick up Jasmine for the Academy, am I right?"

"Yes, ma'am," says Daniel. Bailey chirps her little puppy bark.

"Is this the famous *Bailey* I've been hearing about?" asks Jasmine's mom.

"Is this the famous Bailey I've been hearing about?"

"Yes, she's famous, I guess," you respond. "At least with all the cadets."

"Well, Jasmine is almost ready," her mom continues. "She's having a little difficulty in the backyard with Peanut and Smores. Come on in."

Peanut and Smores? The three of you walk through the house and into Jasmine's backyard. She's running around trying to pick up something small—and *fast*.

"What in the world …?" asks Daniel.

"They're her guinea pigs," says Jason. "And they are almost as cute as your puppy."

"Yes," explains Jasmine's mother, "we let them out of their cage every once in a while to enjoy the freedom of the backyard."

"But it's not easy to get them back in their hutch sometimes!" shouts Jasmine, looking flustered. "Don't just stand there. Help me!"

"Don't just stand there. Help me!"

Before any of you can respond, Bailey pulls free from her make-shift leash and bolts across the yard. She's even faster than Peanut and Smores! She runs directly toward the guinea pigs and starts circling them while barking feverishly. Jasmine and her mother stand in awe and barely know what to do.

"Bailey!" shouts Daniel in an effort to retrieve her. It's no use. Bailey is on a mission, speedily circling back and forth until Peanut and Smores have responded to the pup and are grouped together in the middle of the yard. Once the guinea pigs stop running, Bailey also stops and stands poised, waiting for them to move again.

"Wow," remarks Jason. "It's almost like Bailey's playing a game with them ..."

"Or trying to gather them," you say, as Bailey continues to guard the guinea pigs. Her stub of a tail is wagging proudly.

"Quick, let's get Peanut and Smores back in their hutch!" says Jasmine. Her mom helps her gather the small animals and place them back in a raised, wooden hutch-like cage.

"That was a little easier than usual," says Jasmine. "You can bring Bailey over anytime the guinea pigs are free in the backyard."

Her mom latches the hutch closed. "I bet we could train Bailey to help us put Peanut and Smores away every day!"

"Well," says Daniel, "hopefully we'll find Bailey's owner soon, but if not, I'll be happy to train her to be a guinea pig gatherer."

Daniel reconnects Bailey's leash, and the four of you head out to the police station for the next Academy session.

 As all the cadets enter the briefing room, Detective Jeffries is writing on the whiteboard, and this time it's one word: TRAIN. He finishes, turns around, and sees the look on everyone's faces. "I'm not sure what to make of you today. Are you *eager*, or *anxious*, or ..."

Daniel says, "Eager to find Bailey's real home. And maybe a little anxious too. If I can't solve this mystery soon, I may not *want to solve it at all.* I really like having a dog."

Hannah reaches over and pats his shoulder sympathetically, then says, "I'm eager too. But for me, it's about Tiana, and I'm also frustrated. It's been a few days now and I haven't helped her much. I'm afraid what Marco said to her will start to change the way she thinks about Jesus."

"Let's get at it then," says Detective Jeffries. "You've encountered true *tests* with Bailey, Marco, and Tiana. You've been challenged, and because of that, something special is about to happen."

He turns and starts drawing on the whiteboard. Under the word "TRAIN," to the left he writes the words "Frustrating Test." Then, to the right, again under the word "TRAIN," he writes "Future Task." Finally, he draws an arrow from the left to the right, connecting the two groups of words.

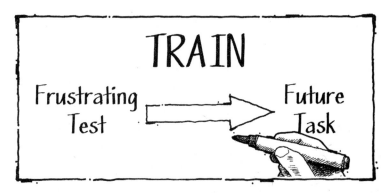

"You started with *frustrating tests*, agreed? You know the challenges and mysteries that you haven't been able to solve so far," he says.

"No one seems to have made any progress with Marco or Bailey," notes Jason, looking back and forth between Daniel and Hannah to see if they would agree.

"Maybe not, but I am confident that you will find Bailey's home and help Tiana and Marco too," says Jeffries as he points to the right of his diagram. "That's the *future task* you're trying to achieve."

Detective Jeffries then points to the thick arrow in his diagram. "This arrow is the good part," he says, smiling. "It's what happens when you discover you *don't* have the answers you want."

The cadets have a puzzled look on their faces.

"Once you know what you don't know, you're motivated to learn. Between the *test* and the *task* is a great opportunity to *train*." Jeffries puts down his marker.

Detective Definitions

Training:

Detectives train so they can get better at doing their job. Training involves putting what you learn into *practice*. Detectives apply what they've learned every day.

As Christians, we also must train. That means we must learn something and then *put it into practice* by *applying* what we've learned.

Can you think of a simple way you can apply what you've learned so far as a Christian?

"You mean like this teaching session we're having today?" asks Jasmine.

"Close," replies Detective Jeffries. "Teaching is similar to training, but there's an important difference. Training has an immediate goal in mind, a challenge we must face in the near future. What's your challenge, Daniel?"

"To find Bailey's owner."

Jeffries turns to Hannah. "And yours?"

"To help Tiana and Marco," she replies.

"Everything you investigate, study, and learn between the challenges you've experienced so far and the success I'm sure you'll achieve will come as the result of *training.*" Detective Jeffries looks up as though he's thinking about something.

"I've had my fair share of frustrating tests," he says. "I had a case as a new detective that I just couldn't solve. I interviewed many people I thought might be my suspect, but I couldn't tell which, if any, was lying. After many weeks I asked my sergeant if I could attend special training that would help me interview suspects to figure out if they were telling the truth. After that training, I was a better interviewer." Detective Jeffries focuses back on the cadets. "I reread all my interviews and eventually figured out who my suspect was. My frustrating *test* motivated me to *train* for the future *task.*"

CSI Assignment

The cadets will eventually be good detectives just like Detective Jeffries.

Read Luke 6:40.

"A pupil is not above his _____;
but everyone, after he has been fully _____, will be like his teacher."

Who is training you as a Christian? Who do you hope to be like one day?

_____

Detective Jeffries asks the cadets, "Have any of you ever experienced something similar?"

The cadets think about his question.

"I remember learning to ride a bike," says Jason. "I couldn't keep my balance! I kept falling off, and I skinned both knees. Then I skinned both elbows. I fell so many times that there wasn't much left to skin!"

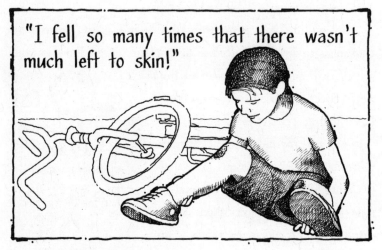

The cadets laugh.

"But I was determined not to let that bike defeat me!"

"Good for you, Jason. Your frustration turned out to be a *good* thing, because it led you to be successful at the task of riding a bike—which, by the way, is really fun. You trained yourself, Jason."

"And after that, I started to learn how to do *tricks* on my bike," adds Jason.

"Something similar is going to happen here," says Detective Jeffries. "You'll solve your mystery and help your friends, and you'll even *exceed your expectations* along the way."

"Will I be able to do *tricks* with my Bible?" quips Hannah.

Jason laughs.

"No need for tricks," says Jeffries. "The truth will speak for itself." Detective Jeffries pulls up a chair again and sits with the cadets. "Hannah, you encountered a true test related to your faith as a Christian. It won't be the first one. You're all going to face challenges. Jesus told us to expect that."

"But why, if Christianity is true?" asks Daniel. "Why would anyone argue against the *truth*?"

"Great question," answers Detective Jeffries. "Some people just need more information. They're not sure because they haven't heard the evidence." He pauses. "But, to be honest, some people don't *want* it to be true."

The cadets are waiting for more.

"Christianity describes the *best* way to live, but it doesn't describe the *easiest* way to live," he says.

"Like loving others as we love ourselves?" Hannah asks. "I've been reading my Bible to help Tiana, and that part of Jesus's teaching stuck out to me. It's not always easy to love people …"

Dig Deep
Visit the Online Academy

Don't forget to keep up with your training sheets at the Case Makers Academy! Keep assembling your Academy Notebook!

"Especially if you don't even like them!" blurts out Jasmine. She looks around at the cadets. They just stare back at her, then break into laughter.

"Exactly," says Detective Jeffries. "Jesus didn't promise us an easy life, but He showed us a better, although harder, way. That's why some people look for reasons *not to believe*."

CSI Assignment

Read Matthew 5:43-45.

"You have heard that it was said, 'You shall love your neighbor and hate your enemy.' But I say to you, _____ your _____ and pray for those who persecute you ..."

Why is this hard for most of us?

_____

Why is it a better way to live, according to the rest of the verse?

_____

Jeffries stands up and points to his diagram. "That's where training comes in. Don't be afraid when unbelievers make claims you can't answer. Christianity is *true*. It can survive the toughest questions. When someone like Marco says something untrue about Christianity and you're not sure how to respond, just say, 'That's interesting. Let me do some research, and I'll get back to you.' Then start *training*."

Detective Jeffries turns with a big smile. "So are you ready to train?"

The cadets respond with a loud "Yes!"

"Okay, here's what you need to do," he says as he writes on the whiteboard.

"First, we need to understand the challenge—the test—as completely as possible." He turns back toward the cadets. "Daniel, what do you know about corgis?"

Daniel looks at Jason, then back at Jeffries. "Not that much, I guess," he says, a little embarrassed that he didn't think of doing some research.

"Okay then, your job is to find out everything you can about corgis." Bailey barks on cue, as if she knows Detective Jeffries is talking about her.

"Hannah," he continues, "how much do you know about Marco's claims about Jesus? Did you talk to him to see where he got that information or why he chooses to believe it?"

Hannah looks similarly embarrassed. "No, but that does sound like it might be important."

A "Tool" for Your Detective Bag!

Enjoy the Tests!

Think back to the last time you faced a difficult challenge. What good thing resulted from the challenge you faced? Now think about what you know to be true as a Christian. Has anyone ever challenged your faith? Don't be afraid of challenges! They are valuable "tests" that can motivate you to become a better Christian case maker. Let each challenge motivate you to become a good detective.

"Yes, here's an important training point," says Detective Jeffries. "Good *investigations* start with good *questions*."

"I don't know anything about dogs," Daniel says.

The Mysteries Deepen

Training Points to a Future Task

"I don't know anything about dogs," Daniel says as the cadets are walking home from the police station. "Where do I start?"

Jason looks at you and then at Daniel as though he should know the answer to his own question. "You're not much of a detective, are you ..." he says with a sly smirk on his face.

"What do you mean?" replies Daniel.

"Remember when I told you about that poster with all the dogs? Remember where I saw it?"

"Your uncle," says Daniel as he recalls their prior conversation. "You said he was an animal doctor!"

"A veterinarian, yeah. His name is Dr. Whiting. Do you want to walk over to his office on Fig Street? It's not far from here. Maybe he can talk with us for a few minutes."

You and Daniel look at each other, then immediately head in that direction. "Great idea," says Daniel. Bailey is running ahead, exploring the sidewalk from side to side and straining at her rope leash.

"Hi, Jason," says Dr. Whiting's receptionist when you arrive at the office. "I haven't seen you in a while." Jason spends a few minutes talking with her as you and Daniel examine the posters in the waiting room, including the one describing corgis.

When Dr. Whiting walks out to greet you, he sets eyes on Bailey and grins. "I love Pembroke Welsh corgis!" he says.

"You love *all* dogs," kids Jason. "And cats. And hamsters and goldfish and parrots."

"Well, that's true. But these little dogs are smart, friendly, and *extremely* curious. Notice the way they explore every little item in a room." Sure enough, Bailey is moving from end to end, looking for something interesting.

"I guess they'd make good detectives," you say.

Dr. Whiting gets a good laugh out of that. "And this one just appeared out of nowhere," says Jason, explaining how they found Bailey at the recreation center. "We're trying to understand how that happened and where she belongs. Can you tell us something about corgis?"

"Well, we can trace them back to the tenth century, and given that Pembrokeshire is in South Wales, it's possible they came to the British Isles with the Vikings. They're hardworking dogs, and they're loyal to their families." Dr. Whiting appears to be thinking deeply for a moment. "I have a detective 'lead' for you three, if you want to do a little more investigating."

Jason and Daniel look as eager as you feel.

"I can give you the phone number and address of a friend of mine who breeds and raises herding dogs, including corgis. He has a farm where he also keeps *sheep*."

"It's possible they came to the British Isles with the Vikings."

As you are visiting Dr. Whiting, Hannah and Jasmine are about to make a visit of their own. Hannah's mom is driving them across town to Marco's house where they will meet Tiana and Marco. When they arrive, Marco is busy on the driveway, removing a large, empty cardboard box from the back of his mom's truck-shaped SUV. He waves hello. Tiana is standing beside him.

"Let's go inside," he says to the three girls. He seems very intent, as if he has a purpose in mind.

"Marco," says Hannah, "if you don't mind my asking, does your mother still seem sad?"

Marco nods and leads them to the family room. "I wanted to show you a book I found," he says, changing the subject. He produces a book with an ancient painting of Jesus on the cover. Hannah looks at it, turns to the back side of the book, and reads the summary.

"I wanted to show you a book I found," he says, changing the subject.

The book's back cover says:

This fascinating new book sets the record straight about Jesus. As a Jewish teacher living in the ancient world, Jesus was responsible for some of the greatest sermons ever given, but his overly enthusiastic followers exaggerated his story and his message. Jesus never claimed to be anything other than a wise man, and he certainly never claimed to be God!

Hannah finishes reading this and looks up at Marco, who is now holding another book: a Bible. "Can you find a verse that says anything different?" he asks. "Did Jesus ever say He was God?" Hannah can tell that Marco is *serious*; he's been thinking about this a lot and he won't budge from his position that Jesus was only a man.

"Christians have been making the case for Christianity for over two thousand years—" she begins.

Marco interrupts, "But different kinds of religious people believe different things about God. What if *everyone* is wrong, *including* Christians?"

Hannah isn't sure what to say. Marco seems so sure, and he even has a book written by someone who seems *equally* sure. No wonder Tiana has begun to have her own doubts.

CSI Assignment

Marco said "different kinds of religious people believe different things about God." But this doesn't mean everyone is right.

Read John 14:6.

"Jesus said to him, 'I am the way, and the _____, and the life; no one comes to the Father _____ Me.'"

According to Jesus, will religions other than Jesus lead you to God?

_____

Hannah thinks about what Detective Jeffries said about frustration and how it trains us. Although she doesn't yet know what to say to Marco, at least she knows where he got the information he's been sharing with Tiana. Hannah also thinks about what Detective Jeffries always says about truth: it wins in the end. So, rather than getting upset, Hannah takes a deep breath.

"Thanks for showing me the book," she tells Marco. "I'm going to do an investigation of my own, now that I know where you learned this." She holds the book in one of her hands. "Can I borrow this for a few days?"

Marco agrees, and Hannah and Jasmine leave Marco's house after promising to return with an answer.

 At the next Academy meeting, Detective Jeffries listens to the two reports and seems pleased. "You gathered a lot of good information," he says. "And you're sticking with it—even when it seems like you're only discovering new information in little bits and pieces. Investigations can be like that sometimes; you have to be patient."

"We thought the information about Vikings was interesting," says Daniel.

You and Jason agree. "We watched a movie once about Vikings and it included dragons and other creatures," says Jason.

"It's similar to what you told us, Jasmine," says Daniel. "About the elves and fairies using corgis as horses …"

Before he can say more, Detective Jeffries gives Daniel that look, like Daniel is starting to trust his imagination more than the facts.

"Hold on a minute," says Jeffries. "Did Dr. Whiting offer any *other* explanation for Bailey's speed or her ability to appear suddenly?"

"Um ..." mumbles Daniel as you look at each other. You can't recall if Dr. Whiting said anything that might explain Bailey's unusual abilities.

Detective Jeffries turns to Jasmine and Hannah. "I'm also very interested in your conversation with Marco. Is he still convinced that Jesus never claimed to be God?"

"Yes, he's still convinced," says Jasmine.

"And he showed us this," says Hannah as she pulls Marco's book from her backpack. She hands the book to Detective Jeffries.

"Yes, I've seen similar books," says Jeffries. He scans the room and sees the expression on several of the cadets' faces. "I know it can be shocking to find that people have written books *against* what Christianity teaches, but that shouldn't surprise you. Like I said before, some people need more information, but others don't *want* it to be true."

He turns to the whiteboard and writes a sentence:

"People can be *sincere*, yet *sincerely wrong*," says Detective Jeffries as he puts down the marker. "Marco might sound convincing, just like the author of this book. But that doesn't mean what they're saying is *true*." Jeffries looks at Hannah and Jasmine. "We still have to figure out if Marco just needs more information, or if he's one of those people who doesn't *want* Christianity to be true."

Hannah nods.

"Do you two remember if Marco said what it was about this book that persuaded him?"

Neither girl can recall anything specific.

"I just remember how certain Marco seemed to be and I remembered what you said about truth holding up—like a really strong oak tree or something."

"That's a good comparison. Christianity is true. That's why it will survive any test we apply to it, even *Marco's* test. So be confident, patient, and calm with him."

Detective Definitions

Deploy:

This word comes from the Latin word *displicare* (meaning "to scatter"). It is used to describe the act of sending out people for a *purpose*.

God wants us to engage our friends and family members as a purposeful act of *deployment*.

How can God deploy you to share the truth of Christianity with others?

Detective Jeffries walks over to a bookshelf at one end of the briefing room and starts to remove notepads from one of the shelves. "I have an important observation I want to share with you, though. None of you seems to have taken any notes during your interviews. You couldn't remember everything Dr. Whiting said about corgis, and you also couldn't remember all of Marco's points about Jesus. Details *matter* and you didn't record any of the details."

You all look at one another, a bit embarrassed.

"This should solve that problem," says Jeffries as he hands out official detective notebooks to all the cadets. "I'm *deploying* you back into the field, and this time, I want you to take notes!"

He writes three instructions on the whiteboard:

Be Thorough
Be Alert
Be Detailed

"As you're taking notes, keep these three things in mind. First, be thorough! Read everything you can and ask every question you can think of. Next, be alert! Remember that *everything* has the potential to be evidence, so don't ignore anything because you think it might be unimportant. Finally, be detailed! Take really good notes so you'll remember every detail later."

The cadets take their new notepads and head for the door.

"Hey, can I get a free pen too?" requests Jasmine with a grin on her face.

"Don't push your luck there, rookie!" replies Detective Jeffries as the other cadets laugh. Daniel hands Jasmine one of his extra pens and hurries her toward the door before Detective Jeffries can say anything else.

A "Tool" for Your Detective Bag!
Show Your Confidence!

In everything you do as a Christian case maker, be confident, patient, and calm. Others will notice your character and will eventually recognize it as the character of *Jesus* shining through you.

"Where's Bailey?" asks Jasmine as she joins you on the front steps of the library.

Determined to Be Detectives

Investigators Take Great Notes

You and Daniel decide to head for the local library to do some serious research on corgis. Because it's near Jasmine's house, Daniel invites her to meet you there.

"Where's Bailey?" asks Jasmine as she joins you on the front steps of the library.

"I didn't think they'd let her come in," says Daniel.

"Besides," you add, "she can't read."

As the three of you walk in and look around, Daniel appears uncertain where to begin.

"Let's ask the librarian," suggests Jasmine as she approaches the main desk. The woman sitting there has a name tag that says

Mrs. Timberly. As she sees you walking toward her, she seems to be reading your minds. "You three look like you could use some help."

"How can we learn about corgis—you know, the dogs?" asks Daniel. He tells the librarian about Bailey and the mystery of where she came from.

"Follow me," she says as she leads you toward the books related to animals. "Here is the dog section, and we also have Internet resources." Mrs. Timberly points to a long desk with several computer terminals.

A few minutes later, you and Daniel bring a few books to the computer table. Jasmine is searching for pictures and websites involving corgis. She's already giggling at what she's found.

"Check this out." She chuckles. It's an image of two corgis wearing human shirt collars and ties.

"Apparently corgis are snappy dressers," adds Jasmine.

"Apparently corgis are snappy dressers."

"Focus, Jasmine … *Focus*," reminds Daniel. "We came here to solve a mystery, remember?" He looks at the picture. You also look at the picture. Then all three of you start laughing.

"Okay, I'll get serious," promises Jasmine. You pull out your note-pads to start taking notes. Several minutes later, Jasmine holds up a book she's been reading. "Hey, I think I've found some answers to our mystery." The cover of the book reads simply *Dogs That Herd*.

 While you're at the library, Jason has joined Hannah to help her find out what Jesus really said about Himself. Detective Jeffries asked them to consult an expert, so Hannah takes Jason to Pastor Woods at her church. The pastor meets them along with his daughter Claire.

"I didn't know you were going to be here!" says Hannah, pleased to see her friend from youth group. Hannah introduces Jason to Claire, as Pastor Woods walks over to his bookshelf. "I don't often get a request like this," he says. "I love it when young people want to learn more about Jesus, and Claire was glad to hear you were coming."

He selects a handful of books from the shelves and stacks them on the desk, creating a tower of thick volumes. Jason glances at Hannah, then at Claire, then back at the books. He has a look on his face that says, "What did I get myself into?"

Pastor Woods sees Jason's expression. "Don't be so frightened! I'm not going to make you read all these books by yourself. I'll help guide you through the evidence, and these books will help us."

Hannah and Jason look at each other and breathe a sigh of relief. "We better take some notes," says Jason.

"I've got a notepad in the other room …" offers Claire. Hannah and Jason are grateful to have her help.

"Great. If you brought your Bibles, I've got a suggestion." Pastor Woods waits for Claire to return, then asks her for her Bible. He opens it and places it next to Jason's notepad. "As you take notes on your notepads, don't be afraid to write *in your Bibles*."

"You mean, on the Bible *pages?*" asks Jason cautiously.

"That's right," says Pastor Woods, removing several colored pens from a drawer in his desk.

"He taught me to do this a long time ago," adds Claire. She opens and shows her Bible, which is filled with colorful notes in all the margins. Several passages are circled and underlined.

"You can use the space next to the verses to write about the evidence you find," continues Pastor Woods.

"I never thought of that," says Hannah.

"It's not 'against the rules' to write in your Bibles," he says. "God is pleased when we take His Word seriously and study it."

They spend the rest of the afternoon using the pens, searching for evidence and circling information. Pastor Woods helps them along the way, referring back and forth to the many books he selected. Claire sits next to Hannah and takes notes for her. "My dad always seems to know exactly where the answers are in Scripture."

"I'm not sure about that," replies Pastor Woods, "but I'm enjoying being a detective today."

 The cadets are eager to share what they've learned at the next Junior Detective Academy session. Daniel brought Bailey along and she's especially playful, running from cadet to cadet, barking as though she'd like them to chase her.

Detective Jeffries calls everyone to attention. "Were you thorough, alert, and detailed? Remember, good detectives do this over and over until it's like a *reflex*," he says. "It's actually like '*muscle memory.*'"

"Our muscles have *memories?*" asks Jason with a quizzical look on his face.

"When you do something repeatedly, you eventually stop thinking about it. You just do it as a matter of *habit*. The same way your body remembers how to ride your bicycle; after riding a few times, you don't even have to think about keeping your balance. Right?"

"It's true," replies Jason. "I just jump on and take off."

"Muscle memory," says the detective. "Good detective habits work the same way. Practice being thorough, alert, and detailed, and after a little while, you'll do it without thinking about it. That's how to become good detectives, and it's also how to become good Christian case makers."

You, Daniel, and Jasmine are eager to tell the group about Pembroke Welsh corgis. Daniel pulls out his notepad and flips through several pages of notes. "Jasmine found a great book on herding dogs. It turns out that corgis were *bred* to be herders."

"What's a herder?" asks Hannah.

"Shepherds use herding dogs to help them gather and control their sheep, cows, horses, or other farm animals," replies Daniel.

"Corgis are great herders because they are *fast*," you add.

"That's because shepherds bred them to be faster and faster over the years," says Jasmine. "And that's not all—shepherds also bred them to be shorter and shorter."

Dig Deep
Visit the
Online Academy

Are you keeping up with the activity and fill-in sheets at the Case Makers Academy? Keep assembling your Academy Notebook!

"Why would they do that?" asks Jason.

"Because short dogs are less likely to be kicked by the animals they herd," you answer.

"Okay, great," says Detective Jeffries. "That's a lot of good information, but tell us how it helps your investigation."

"Well," says Daniel, "this explains why Bailey looks the way she does, and it also explains why she is so fast."

"It also explains why Bailey herded Peanut and Smores like she did," adds Jasmine. "And I guess it makes better sense than the stories about elves and fairies. Bailey seems 'enchanted' at times—she's fast and tiny and incredibly cute—but it turns out that corgis are bred to be this way for a purpose. It's not *incredible*; it's *intentional*."

"Yes, I do think breeding is a better explanation than Viking fantasies," says Detective Jeffries as everyone laughs. "You've learned to think *broadly* about evidence."

"What do you mean by 'think broadly'?" asks Jason.

"It's part of being alert, because *anything* can be used as evidence. Sometimes we look for the most obvious things, and we miss something important that's *hiding in plain sight.*"

"Who would have guessed that a book about *dogs that herd* would help us think correctly about Jasmine's explanation involving elves and fairies?" you say.

"Exactly," replies Detective Jeffries. "Even dog breeding can be used as evidence. We can't just skip over these kinds of details; they're out there for everyone to see, and we don't want to miss them." He turns to Hannah. "Did you find any evidence about Jesus that Marco may not be aware of—you know, maybe something that was *hiding in plain sight?*"

"Well, maybe …" answers Hannah. "Jason joined me, and we visited an expert: one of the pastors at my church, Pastor Woods."

"Good idea," says Jeffries.

"Yes," says Jason. "Maybe *too* good an idea."

Hannah and Jason pull out their notepads and Bibles. The pads look tattered and used. Hannah flips through one of them and shows that nearly every page is full of notes.

Hannah flips through one of them and shows that nearly every page is full of notes.

"Impressive," says Detective Jeffries.

"It gets better," says Jason as he opens his Bible, revealing his multicolored notes on many of the pages of the Gospels. The cadets collectively make an "Oooh …" sound and gather around Jason to get a closer look.

"Pastor Woods told us to use the margins in our Bibles to record some of the evidence we found," says Hannah.

"It sounds like your pastor is a born detective," responds Detective Jeffries. "That's exactly what I do on my investigations when I am studying old case files. I make a copy of each report and start making notes in the margins." Detective Jeffries moves in close and points to one of the Bible pages. "What do the different colors mean?"

"Well," says Jason, "we were trying our best to organize what we found into categories using the different colors. Jesus said and did a lot of things we'd never thought about …"

"Evidence hiding in plain sight?" asks Jeffries.

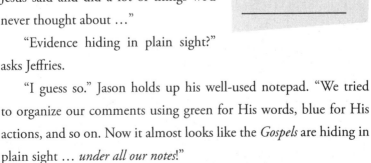

CSI Assignment

Detective Jeffries has been telling the cadets to have patience. Read James 1:2-4. "The testing of your faith produces _____, And let endurance have its perfect result, so that you may be perfect and _____, lacking in nothing." Why do you think knowing the truth can make you a more patient person?

_____

"I guess so." Jason holds up his well-used notepad. "We tried to organize our comments using green for His words, blue for His actions, and so on. Now it almost looks like the *Gospels* are hiding in plain sight … *under all our notes!*"

Detective Definitions

Practices:

Detective Jeffries is training the cadets to follow a detective "process" that will help them solve mysteries. He tells them to be thorough, alert, and detailed and to do this repeatedly until these practices are *habits.*

Detective Jeffries tells the cadets to make these detective practices a part of their "muscle _____"

"Well," Detective Jeffries says with a laugh, "I'm very impressed with your efforts. I gave you careful instructions, and I can see you've followed them. I think you're all about to make a big breakthrough."

The cadets look at each other. "How can you be so sure?" you ask.

"Because I understand the *process*, and you're all approaching the last few steps that detectives take to solve mysteries." Detective Jeffries turns to the whiteboard again. "Are you ready to finish your investigation?"

"Yes!" says everyone before he can say anything more.

"Okay then," says Detective Jeffries as he starts writing.

> 1. Summarize and organize
> 2. Fill in the blanks

"Now I want you to take what you've discovered so far and organize it. Make lists of all the evidence. Maybe even draw some diagrams."

"Diagrams?" asks Jasmine.

"Ask the other cadets," says Jeffries. "I'm sure they remember what they look like from our other Academy sessions, and I'll help you with that in the next session.

"Once you begin to organize your case in this way, you'll be able to figure out what's missing and what you need to do next. You'll be able to *fill in the blanks.*" Detective Jeffries puts down his marker. "I think you're very close."

"It doesn't feel like I'm all that close," says Daniel. "I still don't know where Bailey came from."

A "Tool" for Your Detective Bag!

Be Thorough, Alert, and Detailed!

Good detectives know that anything can be used as evidence to make a case. Be sure to take great notes, and be alert to anything or everything that will help you solve mysteries or make a case. Look for the things that are *hiding in plain sight.* You'll see some examples in the next chapter.

"Trust the process, Daniel," replies Jeffries. "Fill in the blanks. Be creative. Think 'outside the box,' and gather some additional information."

"I've got an idea!" blurts out Jason. "It's not 'outside the box,' but it's definitely *outside.*"

Chapter Six

Getting Close and Getting Organized

Investigators Summarize Their Findings

"Outside?" responds Daniel as he flips through his notepad. "Jason, are you talking about the man with the sheep?"

Jason is also looking through his notes. "His name is Dan Terry. His farm is at 5115 Shady Tree Lane."

"It seems like the logical next step for you," says Jason. "My uncle did say that he raises and sells corgis."

"Wait," interrupts Jasmine. "Do you think …" she says, hopefully. "Do you think Mr. Terry might actually have raised Bailey?"

"If so, that would sure get you close to solving this mystery," says Detective Jeffries.

The cadets leave the briefing room, thinking about the possibilities. Even Bailey seems eager, wagging her stubby tail.

Later that afternoon, Daniel's mom drives you, Daniel, and Jasmine across town to Shady Tree Lane. This part of town is far from Main Street, and there are fewer houses and buildings.

"I like it out here," says Jasmine. "There's a lot of open space."

"It's a good place to raise animals," says Daniel's mom as she pulls up to Mr. Terry's farm. As they walk up the steps to the large, ranch-style house, Bailey starts to jump up and down on her rope leash. Daniel looks at you.

"Are you thinking what I'm thinking?" he asks.

You also sense something different about Bailey's response to Mr. Terry's property. "Do you think she *recognizes* this place?"

"Let's find out," says Daniel.

You knock on the front door of Mr. Terry's house. No one answers the door, even though you and the cadets can hear noises in the house and to the rear of the property.

"Maybe they can't hear us knocking," says Jasmine as she takes the lead and starts to walk around the edge of the house to the backyard. You and Daniel follow her with Bailey pulling eagerly on her leash, as though she knows where she's going.

Behind the house is a large field with kennels, corgis of all ages, and a fenced pasture full of sheep.

Behind the house is a fenced pasture full of sheep.

"Wow, look at this," says Jasmine. "Cute dogs *and* sheep? I want to live here!" She leads everyone to the edge of a corgi pen, where she spots another corgi pup who looks a lot like Bailey. "Look over there. It's amazing how much that puppy looks like Bailey!" You're even more hopeful about this place. Could this be where Bailey came from?

A kind-looking man in work clothes sees your small group and walks up to introduce himself.

"I'm Mr. Terry. Is one of you Jason?"

You look at each other, surprised. How does Mr. Terry know Jason's name?

"No," replies Daniel. "He couldn't come today. How did you know about him?"

"His uncle, Dr. Whiting, told me he might be coming by."

Bailey interrupts with a bark and tugs on her leash, trying to get closer to Mr. Terry. He smiles and reaches out a hand to pet her. "And your name is Bailey, right?"

"And your name is Bailey, right?"

"How do you know her name?" asks Daniel hopefully. "Did you raise her?"

"No, I'm afraid not," says Mr. Terry.

You, Jasmine, and Daniel exhale and are visibly disappointed. "I thought we were close to solving this!" says Jasmine.

"Did you just see the name on her collar?" you ask.

"No … but her collar is the reason why I recognized her," continues Mr. Terry. "Today's not the first time I've seen this dog."

"Really?"

"Bailey came to visit once before, with a woman who was curious about what she should feed a corgi. It looked like she got the puppy on the same day she visited me. Bailey was excited and ran all over the yard, playing with the other corgis. I sold her owner some food and supplies, put it all in a big box, and then I sat down with her and explained all the basics about feeding and raising corgis."

"What was her name?" asks Jasmine eagerly.

"She didn't say, or at least I can't remember if she did."

Detective Jeffries would want you to keep investigating, so together you try to ask good questions and gather all the facts Mr. Terry can remember.

"What did the lady look like?" you ask.

Detective Definitions

Interviews:

Detectives talk to witnesses (and suspects) to get information that will help them solve mysteries. These are more than simple conversations. Interviews are focused and purposeful. They have a goal in mind. What are Daniel and Jasmine's goals in their interview with Mr. Terry?

"Well, she was maybe about forty years old … tall, with long black hair. I think she was wearing jeans, but for sure she was wearing a bright yellow shirt. I remember that. And she was driving a red Jeep."

"A red Jeep?" asks Jasmine. "I've seen one around town; I just can't remember where."

"A red Jeep?" asks Jasmine.

"Me too!" says Daniel.

"That does sound kind of familiar," you add. Jasmine looks at you and Daniel, surprised that you seem to remember the same vehicle.

"Where did we see it?" wonders Daniel.

"I remember the Jeep because she didn't have a dog crate for Bailey yet, and the puppy was running around loosely in the cargo area at the back," Mr. Terry says. "I told her she needed to secure Bailey better than that."

"Hmm. I have another question," says Jasmine. "When this lady bought the supplies, how did she pay?"

Daniel wishes he'd thought of that; after all, a check or credit-card receipt might contain the woman's *name*.

"Let me look," answers Mr. Terry as he enters a shed that contains food, supplies, and a small cash register. Several minutes later he returns with the bad news: Bailey's owner must have paid with cash because Mr. Terry can't find a receipt. Another dead end.

Bailey barks impatiently and strains at her leash. Daniel finally unties her and allows her to run over toward the corgi kennels. She runs from dog to dog, then back to Mr. Terry.

"These little dogs *love* people," he says. "Matter of fact, I have to keep a close eye on them, because not only do they love meeting new people—they're prone to *run off* with them."

As Mr. Terry is rubbing Bailey's stomach, he adjusts her collar. "This collar is what reminded me about Bailey. I think I know where it came from. Have you examined it?"

He unclasps the collar and turns it over. The underside of the collar is stamped with "The Pet Place" in capital letters.

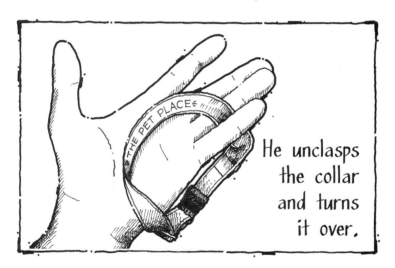

He unclasps the collar and turns it over.

"A store label," says Daniel. "How did we miss that?"

"It was *hiding in plain sight*," replies Jasmine. "It was the only piece of evidence that came with Bailey, and it's been there all along."

 Meanwhile, Jason and Hannah have been sifting through their margin notes for hours. They have that feeling you get before a big test at school, when you think you're ready to pass the test with flying colors. They invite Tiana to Hannah's house to show her what they've discovered so far. They want to make sure they're "A+ ready" before they talk with Marco.

When Tiana arrives, she has a look of relief on her face. "I'm glad you guys called," she says. "I keep thinking about Marco's challenge. Why can't we answer it? I don't know what to think."

"Well," says Hannah, "we've got some new things for you to think about."

Hannah opens up her notepad and shows Tiana everything they collected, as Jason begins a new page of his own to organize the notes into new categories.

Tiana's eyes widen. "Wow!" she says. "Good work."

"We're only halfway through," says Hannah. "Now we're looking for *patterns* in the evidence. Jason is starting a list."

As they go over everything, Tiana's mood begins to lighten. Finally, she says, "You guys are *good*! I've read the Bible in places, but I never noticed all the things you've listed here."

"Don't feel bad," says Jason. "We missed a lot of this evidence too until Pastor Woods helped us see it."

"It was *hiding in plain sight*," says Hannah.

There's a lot to talk about at the next cadet training session. Detective Jeffries is poised at the whiteboard with a marker in his hand.

"We uncovered new evidence," you say.

"Great," replies Jeffries. "Let's start with Bailey's case and list everything we know so far."

You, Daniel, and Jasmine share what you discovered at Mr. Terry's ranch, including the new information about the Pet Place. Detective Jeffries makes a list, summarizing your discoveries about Bailey and her owner:

> Corgis are bred to be fast
> Corgis are friendly by nature
> and like to explore
> Bailey's owner is a woman about
> forty years old
> She has long black hair
> She was wearing a yellow shirt
> and blue jeans
> She was driving a red Jeep
> Bailey wasn't secured in the Jeep
> Bailey was first discovered at the car wash

"That's it!" shout you and Daniel.

"I remember now—the red Jeep was one of the cars at the car wash!" exclaims Daniel.

You agree. "I knew I recognized it when Mr. Terry first described it. It didn't dawn on me until you made this list."

"So, this explains why Bailey first appeared at the car wash," says Hannah. "Her owner must have been there getting her Jeep washed as part of the baseball fundraiser."

You and Daniel nod your heads in agreement.

"But that doesn't explain why Jasmine and I *also* recognized the description of the red Jeep. Neither one of us was at the car wash …"

"Good point," says Detective Jeffries. "Jason, did your team keep a record of who got their cars washed that day at the recreation center?"

"I don't think so," says Jason.

"Well, our summary list did help us organize the evidence and inch closer toward solving the mystery. Don't forget, you still have one more important clue to investigate."

"The Pet Place," you all declare in unison.

 "Exactly. Now let's turn to Hannah and Jason's work on Marco's claims about Jesus."

"Well, Marco is right in one way," says Hannah. "Jesus didn't specifically say, 'I am God.' Not with those exact words, anyway. But He did say things that made it clear that He is God."

"Like what?" asks Detective Jeffries.

"Well," begins Jason, opening up his Bible, "in Matthew 13:41, for example, He talked about sending His angels to gather up all those who commit lawlessness."

"So how does that make it clear that He is God?" asks Jeffries.

"Well," says Hannah, "you taught us a long time ago that every word matters, right?"

"Yes, absolutely."

"He called the angels *His* angels. Only God can send angels, but here Jesus is saying that *He* is going to send the angels …"

"As if Jesus was God and was in charge of the angels," finishes Jason. "And He talks that way in many other places in the Gospels."

"Hmm, very interesting," responds Detective Jeffries. "So, Jesus talks as though He has the *authority* of God."

"Yes, and there's more," says Hannah. "This next piece of evidence was really *hiding in plain sight*. Have you ever noticed that all of God's *human* prophets like Isaiah or Ezekiel or any other Old Testament prophet, when they speak for God they always say something like, 'Thus says the Lord …'?"

"Or, 'The Lord Almighty says …'" adds Jeffries. "Yes, I've noticed that."

"Well, Jesus never, ever says anything like that when He speaks the words of God. Look at Matthew 5:18, for example." Hannah flips through the gospel of Matthew. "Jesus speaks God's words by saying, '*I* tell you the truth …'"

"So, what do you make of that?" asks Jeffries.

CSI Assignment

Jesus claimed that He and God the Father were one.

Read John 14:6-9 (the rest of the verse you started in an earlier chapter).

Look at what Jesus told Philip in verse 9: "He who has seen _____ has seen the _____."

What does this tell us about Jesus?

_____

CSI Assignment

Jesus spoke repeatedly as if He were God. Read Isaiah 10:24. How does Isaiah begin speaking for God?

_____

Now read Mark 11:23. How does Jesus begin speaking as God?

_____

Jason provides the answer. "The prophets speak *for* God, but Jesus speaks *as* God."

"I never noticed that before," declares Hannah, "but now that I'm looking at everything as evidence, it's obvious."

"Like it's been hiding in plain sight all along," says Daniel.

"One more thing," says Jason as he searches his Bible again. "Jesus even called Himself the 'I am.'"

"I don't understand," remarks Jasmine. "He called Himself *what*?"

Hannah opens the Old Testament part of her Bible. "God told Moses to call Him 'I am'; God identified Himself with that name to all the Israelites."

"Seems like an unusual name," responds Jasmine.

"God is the only one who was ever called that," replies Jason. "Until Jesus came along."

Hannah opens the New Testament part of her Bible. "Check this out. In John's gospel, chapter 8, Jesus called Himself the 'I am' several times. Jesus even said, 'Before Abraham was, I AM.'"

"That's a bold statement," says Detective Jeffries. "Abraham was the ancient father of the Israelites, and Jesus said that He existed even *before* Abraham. It does sound like Jesus is calling Himself God."

Hannah adds, "When Jesus said that, the religious leaders wanted to put Him to death, because they knew this was exactly what He meant."

Detective Jeffries gives Hannah and Jason a thumbs-up. "Now let's summarize your findings":

> ## Jesus claimed the authority of God
> ## Jesus spoke as if He is God
> ## Jesus referred to Himself with the same name as God
> ## (the "I am" statements)

"That sounds like strong evidence." Detective Jeffries hands the marker to Jason. "Do you think you could draw this in diagram form?"

Jason steps up to the whiteboard and takes several minutes to draw a diagram. Hannah adds the verses from the Bible:

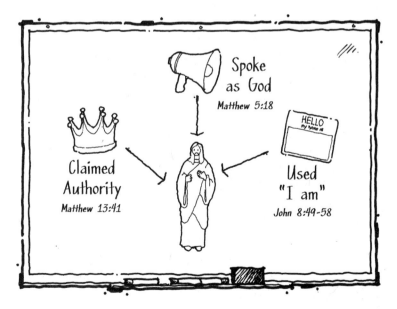

Spoke as God
Matthew 5:18

Claimed Authority
Matthew 13:41

Used "I am"
John 8:49-58

A "Tool" for Your

Detective Bag!
Organize Your Evidence!

After you've taken good notes and gathered as much evidence as possible, start grouping the pieces of evidence together in categories that will help you make the case, just like Detective Jeffries did in this chapter.

Use lists and diagrams to group what you discover. Keep your lists in a place where you can find them and refer to them in the future.

"Wow," remarks Daniel. "When you see it like that, it sure seems like Jesus said He was God."

"Yes," says Hannah. "He might not have used the exact words 'I am God,' but at the time, everyone understood what He was saying, that's for sure."

Detective Jeffries admires Jason and Hannah's diagram. "I think you're ready to make the case to Marco, and I bet Tiana would be willing to go with you. The final step in any investigation is making the case to a jury, and Marco is the jury this time around."

Jeffries turns to you, Daniel, and Jasmine. "Meanwhile, the three of you have a lead to chase down, right?"

You say, "The Pet Place—we're on it!"

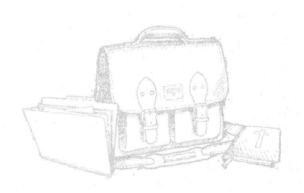

What Should We Say?

Communicators Think About Their "Jury"

"Let's get this case solved!" says Hannah as you all meet at Daniel's house. Everyone starts walking toward the Pet Place, with Bailey happily trotting along ahead of you at the end of her leash. Once you arrive, Mrs. Stallings, who owns the store, recognizes Bailey immediately. "I'm happy to see this little beauty again," she says. Bailey responds accordingly and rolls over on her back.

"Amazing," says Jasmine as she looks around the shop. There are all kinds of interesting animals chirping, purring, cooing, and barking. "Are those guinea pigs?" she asks, pointing to a pen in the far corner of the shop.

"No," replies Mrs. Stallings, "they're a litter of bunnies."

Jasmine can hardly contain herself. "Are they old enough for me to hold?"

"Sure, they're *very* friendly."

Jasmine opens the gate of the hutch and gently removes one of the bunnies. "They're even softer than Peanut and Smores."

Dig Deep
Visit the Online Academy

If you've been keeping up with the online materials at Case Makers Academy, you're almost ready to graduate! Be sure to complete your activity sheets.

"Peanut and Smores?" asks Mrs. Stallings.

"Those are her guinea pigs," explains Jason.

Bailey is wagging her stubby tail uncontrollably and barking at the sight of the bunny in Jasmine's arms. The small bunny, startled by the barking, jumps from Jasmine's grasp and bolts across the floor of the pet store.

Bailey breaks away from Daniel's grasp, and the chase is on!

"Oh no!" shouts Mrs. Stallings. Everyone scrambles to catch Bailey and the bunny. Jasmine chases after Bailey, leaving the bunny pen open behind her. Before anyone even notices, all the other bunnies jump out of the hutch and start hopping across the shop floor.

Bailey is as fast as ever, escaping the control of everyone in her effort to joyfully herd the stray bunnies. Jason and Daniel stop for a minute, out of breath, and look at the chaos.

Daniel hears a new noise to his left and sees a small pen of kittens. The pen is tall but has no covering on the top. "Oh no," says Daniel.

Before he can do anything about it, several of the kittens, spooked by the noise in the shop, leap out of the pen and bolt across the store. Unlike the bunnies, the kittens aren't limited to the floor of the shop. They easily jump, climb, and scurry across counter and shelf tops.

They jump, climb, and scurry across counter and shelf tops.

"Are you kidding me?" asks Daniel. "Can this get any crazier?" He runs toward the nearest kitten, hoping to grab it.

Jason is so stunned that he hardly knows what to do. Suddenly, he hears a loud squawking sound behind him. "Hello! Hello! Hello! Hello!" He turns around and sees two very large parrots sitting on perches. Each has a name tag attached to its perch: Tarzan and Jane.

"Uh, Daniel?" Jason stammers. "I think it's going to get crazier ..." Sure enough, the parrots join the chaos by trying to fly from their perches. With their wing feathers clipped, the best they can do is take short flights from shelf to shelf, and counter to counter.

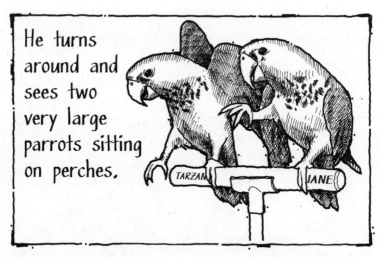

He turns around and sees two very large parrots sitting on perches.

You stand in the middle of this turmoil, watching as bunnies and kittens dart from place to place, parrots fly from end to end, and Bailey does her best to herd everyone, including *the cadets.*

Daniel makes a quick decision to grab Bailey. He stomps his foot on the leash trailing behind her and reels her in. The chaos in the room begins to settle a bit, and within minutes, Daniel is holding Bailey, Jasmine is cradling an armload of bunnies, you and Jason have a parrot on each hand, and Hannah and Mrs. Stallings are holding several kittens. Everyone's hair is messed up, and Jason's and Daniel's shirts are untucked. Several items have fallen from the shelves and are littered across the floor.

"I wish I had a camera …" says Mrs. Stallings, "or a free hand to use one—this is the funniest sight I've ever seen."

Everyone laughs and takes a deep breath. After all the pets are returned and the aisles cleaned up, Daniel apologizes for the ruckus and finally gets around to the reason you all are there in the first place.

"This is the funniest sight I've ever seen."

"Mr. Terry, the corgi breeder, recognized Bailey's collar as coming from your store," he says as he removes the collar and shows Mrs. Stallings the label.

"Yes, that's one of our collars," she replies as she straightens her hair and looks carefully at Bailey's name embroidered on the outside of the collar. "Sometimes customers ask to have the pet's name

"Yes, that's one of our collars."

embroidered, or sometimes a family name. Our machine can do it while they wait."

"Do you remember Bailey's owner?"

Mrs. Stallings thinks for a minute. "Well, I remember she had a really bright gold blouse. It was pretty—with ruffles at the cuffs of the sleeves. She was younger than me, I think, maybe forty-five years old. And she had long, curly black hair."

"Do you remember what kind of pants and shoes she wore?" asks Jason, trying to be thorough.

"Hmm ... I'm not sure. She might have been wearing a skirt."

Jasmine takes Hannah aside and whispers to her, "This description is a little different than the one we got from Mr. Terry."

Detective Definitions
Reliable Eyewitnesses:

Two witnesses aren't likely to agree on every detail. This doesn't mean they can't be trusted. Good detectives do their best to understand how two people can see the same thing yet describe it differently.

Why might Mrs. Stallings's and Mr. Terry's descriptions of Bailey's owner be slightly different?

"That's not unusual," replies Hannah. "Detective Jeffries taught us about this in a prior Academy. Witnesses don't usually agree about everything. It doesn't mean they are lying; in fact, you should be suspicious if the witness *do* agree about every detail. It's natural for two or three witnesses to describe things slightly differently."

"I guess that makes sense," says Jasmine, "and it does sound like Mrs. Stallings is talking about the same woman described by Mr. Terry."

"Did Bailey's owner pay with a check or credit card?" asks Daniel.

He looks over at Jasmine, proud of the fact he learned this question from her earlier.

As Mr. Terry did, Mrs. Stallings sifts through her receipts for the past several days but can't find anything related to the collar. "She must have paid cash."

"Oh well," sighs Jason. "We tried." Jason is frustrated that no new information has been discovered from Mrs. Stallings. "Is there anything else you can remember about Bailey's owner?" he asks finally, a little bit desperate.

"Yes, there is one thing," answers Mrs. Stallings. "The lady told me that she had just purchased this little pup for her son."

Daniel is delighted with the new information, and he's writing everything down in his notepad. "Did she tell you her son's name?"

"No, she didn't," says Mrs. Stallings.

Daniel is disappointed but thanks Mrs. Stallings for her patience, both with their questions and with the turmoil Bailey caused in the store.

Everyone is startled again by sudden squawking: "Good-bye! Good-bye! Good-bye! Good-bye!"

"I think Tarzan and Jane are ready to take a nap," explains Mrs. Stallings.

"It has been a real *jungle* in here today," replies Jason.

You and the rest of the cadets groan at Jason's pun as Daniel leads Bailey out of the store.

 Back at the briefing room, Daniel shares the additional bit of information with Detective Jeffries and tells him about the chaos Bailey caused at the Pet Place.

Detective Jeffries is amused by Daniel's description and congratulates the cadets for learning more about Bailey's owner. "Little by little, you're inching closer to the answer." Jeffries then returns to the whiteboard and picks up a marker.

"Once you've investigated something, it's time to tell others about what you've discovered, and good communicators do two things. First, they learn as much as they can about their audience, then they prepare them to hear the truth":

TO BE A GOOD COMMUNICATOR...
1. Know who you are talking to
2. Teach them the truth
   about evidence

"In our case involving Marco, Tiana took a great first step. She cared about Marco and spent time talking with him":

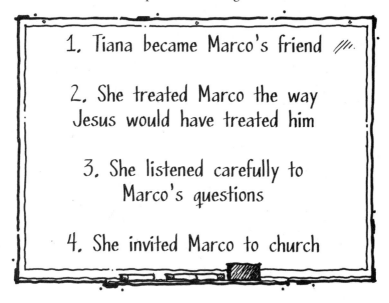

1. Tiana became Marco's friend ////.

2. She treated Marco the way Jesus would have treated him

3. She listened carefully to Marco's questions

4. She invited Marco to church

"Most of us can do at least one of these four things with our friends too," observes Detective Jeffries.

"That seems easy enough," replies Hannah.

"Once you've learned something about Marco and befriended him, it's important to help him be a good detective." Detective Jeffries points to his second guideline for good communicators. "If Marco doesn't know some basic rules of evidence, he may not understand what you're telling him about Jesus."

Jeffries now starts a new list:

"Tiana became Marco's friend. Now it's *your* turn to teach him about evidence." Detective Jeffries turns to the cadets. "First, help Marco understand that just because someone's written a book

RULES ABOUT EVIDENCE

1. Just because someone writes something in a book, it doesn't mean it's true

2. Everything has the potential to be evidence

3. The more cumulative the case, the more reasonable the conclusion

claiming that Jesus never said He was God, this doesn't mean the book is *telling the truth*."

"But Marco said the author was an expert," answers Hannah.

"Maybe," responds Jeffries. "But the author may be one of those people who refuses to listen to the truth. Even smart people do that occasionally. He might have written a book that *sounds* correct, even though it *isn't*. What matters most is the strength of his evidence, not the fact that he wrote it in a book, no matter how important it might look."

"Hmm, now I see what you mean," says Hannah.

"Next, help Marco understand that even the smallest words used by Jesus are important to understanding what Jesus said about Himself. Encourage Marco to consider every word closely."

"Like when Jesus spoke as though He was God?" asks Jason.

"Exactly. Last thing: help Marco understand what a 'cumulative case' is all about."

"Cumulative?" asks Jasmine. "What does that mean?"

"When several different kinds of evidence point to the *same answer*," replies Jeffries, "you've probably got the *right answer*. Help Marco to see that the case you are presenting is built on three different kinds of evidence. That's why it's a good case."

"Got it," says Jasmine.

"But after you've taught Marco all of this, I want you to be prepared for something," continues Jeffries. "Even if you do a great job telling Marco the truth about Jesus, he *still* might not listen to what you have to say. Remember, he might be just like the author of the book—not everyone is willing to hear the truth."

Detective Definitions

Cumulative Case:

A case is "cumulative" when it includes many pieces of evidence pointing to the same conclusion. Three pieces of evidence, for example, are more powerful than one.

Think back to chapter 6 and list the three kinds of evidence Hannah and Jason can use to show that Jesus said He was God:

_____

"Remember, not everyone is willing to hear the truth."

"What can we do if Marco doesn't accept what we have to say?" asks Hannah.

"Remember your duty, and *continue to make the case*," answers Jeffries. "Even if he doesn't agree with you, and if that happens, be sure to rely on the most important tool you have when sharing Jesus with others ..."

"What's that?" asks Jasmine.

"The power of God," replies Detective Jeffries. "Whenever I'm sharing with someone who doesn't seem interested, I *pray* and continue to *show them what Jesus is like by the way I act around them*. God can answer my prayers—and use my example of Jesus—to change their heart. I have to trust Him for that."

"Do you think God can do that with Marco?" asks Hannah. "Sometimes when I'm talking with him, it feels like *nothing* can change his mind."

"Yes, Hannah," says Jeffries. "I *know* it's possible, because it happened to *me*."

Everyone sits quietly, waiting for Jeffries to continue.

"When I was younger, I had my mind made up about God. I didn't believe He existed and no one could convince me otherwise."

"What happened?" asks Daniel.

"One day I had a change of heart. I decided to be open and fair about the evidence—I became *interested*. I was surprised that I was even willing to examine the evidence, and

CSI Assignment

Good communicators show others what Jesus is like.

Read Colossians 3:12-15.

These verses tell us how to live and behave like Jesus. According to verse 14, what one characteristic of Jesus are we to "put on" beyond all others?

the people who knew me were also surprised. I eventually investigated the case for God and became a Christian. Years later I learned that people had been praying for me long before I had that change of heart."

Jeffries stops and smiles at Hannah, then says, "That's why I know God can soften Marco's heart as well."

"Okay," declares Hannah. She takes a deep breath. "I think we're ready."

"I *know* you're ready," encourages Detective Jeffries. "But I'm going to give you one last super-secret piece of detective advice. Are you ready?"

The cadets are quietly listening. Detective Jeffries writes a short sentence on the whiteboard:

TO BE A GOOD COMMUNICATOR...
1. Know who you are talking to
2. Teach them the truth
   about evidence
3. DON'T BE BORING!

The cadets laugh. "That's it?" you say. "Don't be boring? That's your '*super-secret detective advice*'?"

"Yup," says Jeffries. "Start with *enthusiasm*. If *you* don't seem interested in what you've learned, *Marco* won't be interested *either*. Practice what you're going to say, even if only in your minds. Then, *get excited!* God's using *you* to share the truth with Marco!"

A "Tool" for Your Detective Bag!

Know and Help Your Listeners!

When you share the truth about Jesus with your friends or family members, take your time with them, care about their well-being, and learn all you can about them.

Then teach them something about how we use evidence to figure out what is true.

Listen carefully, pray often, and help your listeners understand.

"That *is* pretty amazing if you think about it," replies Hannah.

"Then finish *well*," continues Jeffries. "Use every piece of information you can think of. Draw your diagram for him, let him see your lists, and show him all those colorful notes in your Bibles. Make sure he knows how powerful the case is."

"Let's do it!" shouts Jason. "You remind me of our baseball coach right before a big game!"

"I want you to be as enthusiastic about this as you are to play in the championship game," says Detective Jeffries. "But remember that once you make the case, it's up to Marco to decide if he thinks it's true or not. You can't make that decision for him, and you can't get upset if he doesn't agree with you. Your job is to make the case. After that, Marco must make his *own* decision."

"I'm already praying Marco will be open to the evidence," says Hannah.

"Me too," adds Detective Jeffries. "Me too."

You walk together, still laughing about what happened at the Pet Place.

A Surprising Discovery and a Mystery Solved

Communicators "Get in the Game"

 Jason and Hannah spend the evening practicing what they are going to say, and everyone agrees to meet after school the next day to visit Marco. Hannah makes the phone call, and Marco says it's okay for them to come over. Tiana will be there too.

"Let's take Bailey," Daniel says. "She would enjoy the exercise."

Hannah rings the doorbell at Marco's house. Bailey sits patiently on the customized doormat displaying a large "B" in the center.

"Come on in," says Marco as he opens the door. Tiana is already there, standing behind Marco.

Marco's face lights up as he sees Bailey. "You brought a puppy!" he says. "I've always wanted a corgi—it's my favorite kind of dog."

As you enter Marco's living room, you can smell the sweet scent of something baking in the kitchen. Birthday decorations adorn the

"I've always wanted a corgi— it's my favorite kind of dog."

walls. Tiana explains, "Tomorrow is Marco's birthday. His mom is in the kitchen baking a cake." No wonder the room smells so good!

Hannah takes the lead. "Marco, you got us interested in studying what Jesus said about Himself. Is it all right if we sit down and show you what we've learned?"

"Sure. Why don't we use the dining room table?"

Even before you're all seated at the table, you've been praying that God would help Marco see the truth. As you look at the other cadets, you wonder if they're also silently praying.

Tiana sits down to the right of Marco, anxious to see how he will react. Since her last meeting with Hannah and Jason, her confidence in the Christian faith has grown, and she feels certain Jesus really did claim to be God.

Jason does exactly as Detective Jeffries suggested and starts off by teaching Marco something about evidence. He is eager, and you can *feel* his enthusiasm. "Marco, we've been training at the Junior Detective Academy, studying evidence, and learning how it can be used to make a case."

Marco's eyebrows raise slightly as he shifts in his chair.

Hannah continues, "We've learned that people can say all kinds of things, but just because someone writes something in a book, that doesn't mean it's true. It all depends on how strong the evidence is."

"And all kinds of things can be considered as evidence," adds Jason, "including even the smallest action or word."

Detective Definitions

Opening Statement/ Closing Argument:

When attorneys make a case in court (in front of a jury), they give an opening statement *before* showing all the evidence, and then a closing argument *after* showing the evidence. They prepare these presentations carefully.

We can also prepare before we share the truth about Jesus. If someone asked why you're a Christian, what would you say?

"So, we've read through all the Gospels and collected all the words that Jesus used to describe Himself," says Hannah. "The case is large, and we think it's powerful."

Hannah shares her notes with Marco, and he appears impressed with all the colored notations in her Bible. Jason carefully draws his diagram, laying out the three kinds of evidence they used to make their case. They are gentle, respectful, and enthusiastic. They ask questions in certain places and patiently answer Marco's questions along the way.

As they are finishing up, Hannah says, "Marco, I still remember something you said when we first met: 'If Jesus didn't think He was

"The case is large, and we think it's powerful."

CSI Assignment

Jesus said He was God, and then He proved it by rising from the grave.

Read 1 Corinthians 15:3-8.

Paul wrote that Jesus "was _____, and that He was _____ on the third day according to the Scriptures, and that He appeared to _____, then to the twelve. After that He appeared to more than _____ brethren at one time."

God, why should anyone else?' We think it's clear that Jesus really *did* claim to be God, based on all the ways He talked about Himself. And He proved He was God when He rose from the grave!"

Marco pauses, then says something that disappoints you: "I still don't believe Jesus is God. You guys did a great job with all those Bible verses, but I am just not convinced. I still don't believe in God."

Detective Jeffries told you it might turn out this way, and he also encouraged you to let Marco make up his own mind. Hannah checks to be sure that she's answered all of Marco's questions, and when she's done, everyone sits quietly.

Jason breaks the silence. "Marco, I haven't been a Christian long. In fact, not that long ago, I didn't believe in God *at all.*" He pulls his Bible out of his backpack and shows it to Marco. "My grandfather was a believer. This was his Bible; now it's mine."

"I became a cadet at the Junior Detective Academy *before* I was a believer. I didn't really *want* God to exist back then, because my grandfather suffered before he died, and I didn't think God should have allowed that. But I became a believer after I looked at evidence in the universe. I finally realized that God was the only reasonable explanation for that evidence. I would be happy to share what I learned with you if you want to meet again."

Before Marco can respond, his mother enters the room. She's a tall woman in her forties with long black hair.

"My puppy! Who found my puppy?" she cries out.

Everyone is shocked, including Marco.

"She's … *yours?*" stammers Daniel.

"Yes, yes … *Yes!*" she says as she bends down and cradles Bailey in her arms. "Thank you, thank you, thank you for bringing her back to me!"

Bailey licks her neck and face joyfully.

"I never thought I would see her again and I have been depressed for *days*," she continues. "I bought her for Marco for his birthday. He's always loved our friend's corgi, so when she had her own litter of puppies, I decided to bring the last one home to Marco. Believe it or not, I lost this little cutie somewhere on the way home!"

The cadets are still in a state of shock.

"After I picked her up, I stopped at a pet store to get her a collar with our family name on it—"

"Wait," interrupts Daniel. "Your *family* name?"

"Bailey," she replies, pointing to the name on the collar.

"That's their last name," confirms Tiana. "This is *Mrs.* Bailey, and this is *Marco* Bailey."

"Oh my," says Hannah. "Marco, I had no idea your last name was Bailey."

"After I got the collar," Mrs. Bailey continues, "I drove to a special corgi breeder who showed me what kind of food I should feed

her. He also gave me some great tips on raising a 'herding' dog, and he even gave me a large cardboard box to take her home."

"I didn't know that box had a puppy in it," says Marco as he recalls removing the box from his mom's car.

"I didn't want you to know that I lost the puppy," says Mrs. Bailey as she opens the door to the garage. "So, I hid the dog food here in the garage before I asked you to remove the box." Marco can now see the large bag of dog food peeking out from behind a storage tub. The cadets can also see Mrs. Bailey's vehicle, a red Jeep.

"*That's* why we all remembered seeing the Jeep, and it's also why we couldn't remember *where* we saw it!" says Daniel.

"Yes, it's because we *weren't all together* when we saw it!" replies Hannah. "You saw it at the car wash and we saw it here in the driveway."

"The car wash!" blurts out Mrs. Bailey. "Now I recognize you!" She points to you, Jason, and Daniel. "I stopped there after the

The cadets can also see Mrs. Bailey's vehicle, a red Jeep.

breeder. I should have gone straight home, but I still needed to get some gas and to drop off some things at the post office. When I saw your car wash, I wanted to help support your team."

"Now we remember your Jeep as well," you say as Marco and Mrs. Bailey cradle Bailey and enjoy her affection.

"By the time I got home and checked the big box, I saw that the puppy was missing. I drove back to the gas station, the post office, and the recreation center, but your team was already gone, and everything was cleaned up."

"That's why you've been so upset, Mom?" asks Marco.

"Yes," she admits. "I called the local animal shelter, but they said no one turned in a corgi puppy."

Daniel and Jason explain the arrangement they had with Officer Bargar. "That's why Bailey wasn't at the shelter."

All the pieces to the puzzle have fallen into place. Marco's mom fits the description offered by Mr. Terry and Mrs. Stallings, and her Jeep matches the vehicle description. Bailey must have escaped her box as one of the baseball players was washing Mrs. Bailey's car. Even the "B" on the doormat makes sense now.

Trying not to interrupt each other, the cadets quickly stammer out an explanation of the "case" they've been investigating.

Mrs. Bailey is fascinated. "You were visiting *Marco* while the puppy was visiting *you*." She laughs.

Everyone's delighted to have solved the case, but Daniel can't help but be a little sad. He loves the corgi pup, but he also sees the joy in Marco's eyes.

Detective Definitions

Closing a Case:

Once detectives believe they have solved a mystery, they write a report to close the case, listing all the evidence and reasons why they believe they have solved it.

Make a short list of the reasons why the cadets now know who Bailey's owner is:

_____

It's difficult to surprise Detective Jeffries, but he has to admit he didn't anticipate this outcome. As the cadets tell him all about Marco and Bailey, he can only shake his head.

"How did we get so far in our investigation without connecting the dots between Marco Bailey and a puppy with the same name?" he asks.

"Tiana was the missing link," says Hannah. "She was the only one who happened to know Marco's last name, but she didn't know anything about the puppy part of our investigation."

"And what about Marco?" asks Jeffries, changing the topic. "What did he think of your investigation of *Jesus*?"

For a few seconds, no one says anything. Then Jason breaks the news: "He seemed the same as before. He still seems to believe that book of his more than the Bible—or any of our evidence."

Detective Jeffries can see how disappointed everyone is.

"But we prayed about it," says Daniel.

"I prayed the entire time we were there," you add.

"So why didn't God answer our prayers?" asks Hannah.

"God always answers prayers," replies Detective Jeffries, "but the answer isn't always 'Yes.' Sometimes it's 'No,' and sometimes it's 'Not yet.' Maybe that's what God is saying about Marco."

The cadets still look unsatisfied.

"Some of you play baseball, right?"

You, Daniel, and Jason nod in agreement.

"Then you should know how this works," says Jeffries as he returns to the whiteboard. "Sharing the truth about Jesus isn't like a game of tennis. You're not alone on one side of the net, trying to play a perfect game, without anyone else to help you."

He draws a baseball diamond on the board.

"Sharing the truth about Jesus is more like a baseball game. I know everyone wants to hit a home run, but that doesn't happen very often."

"It sure didn't happen with Marco," says Jason.

"It's true that he didn't agree with you or accept what you had to say, if that's what you mean by a 'home run,'" continues Jeffries. "But there are more ways to score than home runs."

"That's for sure," recalls Daniel. "I once drove in a run by hitting a bunt, and to be honest, I hit the bunt *by accident!*"

CSI Assignment

Hannah and Jason aren't the only ones who have a duty to share the truth about Jesus.

Read Matthew 28:19-20.

What does God want us to do with people from "all the nations"?

_____

What does God want us to teach them?

_____

"I remember that game!" says Jason.

"And I bet that happened because the runner was already on third base, right?" asks Detective Jeffries.

"That's right," answers Daniel.

"That's my point. You never know where someone is standing when you share the truth about Jesus. Maybe they're like Marco, standing on first base with a long way to go until they cross home plate. Maybe they're on third, just waiting for someone to bunt them home."

Detective Jeffries draws runners on his diagram. "Your job is to get up to the plate and do your best. Take a swing. Don't be afraid. Try to *make contact with the ball.* You might hit a home run, and score, or you might advance a runner from first to second base, or from second to third base."

"I'm not sure I understand," says Jasmine.

Detective Jeffries explains, "When you're telling someone about Jesus, you never know where they are on their journey. Maybe they're like Marco, just starting out, or maybe they've been thinking about this for a long time. Other people may have shared something about Jesus, and like a baseball player, they're standing on a base somewhere between first and home plate."

"They're standing on a base somewhere between first base and home plate."

Detective Jeffries turns his attention to Hannah and Jason. "You may not have hit a home run with Marco, but you might have hit a single. And by offering to share more with him later, Jason, you still have a chance to step up to the bat."

"I hope so," says Jason.

"God can still use you to help Marco run the bases," assures Detective Jeffries. "And who knows, you might even be there someday to see him cross home plate—just as you've all been praying."

"So that's what you meant by God answering 'Not yet,' then?" asks Jasmine.

"Exactly. You never know what God might do in Marco's life. Clearly God is using you, and maybe it's only the first inning!"

A "Tool" for Your Detective Bag!

Be Part of the Team!

Everyone can do something to help grow the kingdom of God. You may not think you have all the answers, but you can help someone take a small step toward the truth.

Don't be afraid to try. Remember, you don't have to hit a home run, but you do have a duty to step up to the plate and take a swing.

Get in the game: share the truth of Jesus with someone today.

The top rail of the sheep pen
fence feels cool in your hand.

Called to Protect the Truth
Life as a Sheepdog

The top rail of the sheep pen fence feels cool in your hand as you watch one of Mr. Terry's corgis herd sheep from one side to the other. This corgi is fully grown, and he seems to be an expert at controlling the movement of the flock.

"Pretty impressive," says Detective Jeffries.

Officer Bargar is standing next to him. "Yes, very impressive."

Jasmine and the other cadets are watching as well. "I still wish I could live here," says Jasmine. The ranch is filled with the sound of farm animals. Dogs are barking, and sheep are bleating in the background.

"What do you think?" asks Daniel as he walks up from behind the group. Everyone turns and sees him standing with his parents and Mr. Terry. He's holding the small corgi pup that looked like Bailey. "Do you remember this little guy?" he asks you and Jasmine.

"I sure do!" says Jasmine, recalling him from their first visit to the ranch.

"Well, he belongs to Daniel now," says Mr. Terry.

It took some convincing, but Daniel's parents agreed to bring home a corgi puppy, especially after seeing how responsible Daniel was with Bailey. Everyone crowds around the puppy in Daniel's arms.

"And look," says Daniel. "We even got a real leash!" Daniel's dad shows them a brand-new braided leash.

"Can you guess where we bought it?" asks Daniel's mom.

"The Pet Place!" says nearly everyone in unison.

"You're thinking like detectives," says Detective Jeffries.

"I'm impressed with your investigative skills from start to finish," says Officer Bargar. "You solved the mystery and found Bailey's owners."

"Well," says Hannah, "we were actually making a case for Jesus and kind of solved the mystery of Bailey *by accident.*"

"I guess we *were* pretty lucky ..." says Daniel.

"Maybe," replies Jeffries. "But someone once described luck as the intersection of *preparation* and *opportunity.* You all worked hard to investigate Bailey's case—you were *prepared.* So, when the *opportunity* came to put all the pieces together, you were *ready.*"

Dig Deep
Visit the Online Academy

Now that you've finished the academy, be sure to assemble your notebook and print out your graduation certificate at CaseMakersAcademy.com!

"I learned a lot," admits Jason.

"There's one more thing you can learn now," continues Detective Jeffries. "And it's not from me."

All the cadets look around to see who Jeffries is talking about.

"Out there." Detective Jeffries points to the sheep pen. "You can learn something from *this corgi.* Corgis and other sheepdogs are very important. They don't just guide and herd; they *protect* the flock from wolves and other threats."

"Fast, friendly, curious, *and* protective," says Mr. Terry. "They're critical to shepherds."

The detective says, "It's fascinating how the Bible describes us as believers. We are called 'sheep': created by God, but helpless and tending to wander off and get into trouble. Jesus is described as the 'Good Shepherd.'"

"It makes more sense now that we've seen what sheep are like," says Jasmine.

CSI Assignment

Detective Jeffries knows his Bible!
Read Isaiah 53:6.
"All of us like _____ have gone _____ …"
Read 2 Timothy 1:14.
"_____, through the Holy Spirit who dwells in us, the _____ which has been entrusted to you."

"Even though we're described as sheep, we're also called to 'guard the truth'—to guide and protect the truth from wolves and threats, just like sheepdogs guide and protect these sheep."

"The way we helped Tiana?" asks Jason.

"Exactly. She's in Jesus's flock, and she was confused by the claims in Marco's book until you guided her back to the truth. Plus, you got to share truth with Marco. Someday he might also thank you for guiding him to Jesus."

"So, we're like *detective* sheepdogs?" asks Hannah, and everybody laughs.

"That's not a bad way to think about it," says Jeffries. "We accept our duty and train ourselves to investigate the truth so we can share it with others. We're sheepdogs, and we're Christian case makers."

Daniel's new puppy barks in agreement.

INSTRUCTIONS FOR USING THE WEBSITE

Be sure to visit www.ForensicFaithforKids.com with your parents to watch the videos for each chapter, download the Fill-In and Activity Sheets, and learn how to earn your Academy Graduation Certificate.

As part of your academy training, be sure to complete the Fill-In Sheets for each chapter.

Here are a few samples:

Chapter 1 Note Sheet - What Is "Faith" Anyway?
Forensic Faith for Kids

Who is Tiana's friend? _____

Tiana tells Hannah, "He _____ a lot, and he says he's
even read all the gospels to learn what they teach about
Jesus... He said that he thinks Jesus was just a smart
_____. Nothing more. In fact, he said that after
reading the gospels, he couldn't find a single place where
Jesus ever said, '_____'"

How does Hannah respond to Tiana about Marco's objection?
Why does Hannah seem so calm? _____

Why does Detective Jeffries tell the cadets to read
1 Peter 3:15?

_____

_____

"This verse commands us to be able to give the _____
for the _____ we have in Jesus. God wouldn't ask us
to do this if there weren't any good reasons to
_____."

Detective Jeffries describes three different
definitions for the word, "faith." Fill-in the
chart to the right from the chart offered in the
book:

"Jurors make a decision based on _____,
even though they have some _____
questions. That's what a good, '_____
faith' is all about."

UNREASONABLE FAITH	BLIND FAITH	FORENSIC FAITH
"_____" the evidence	"_____" any evidence	"_____" the evidence

A "Tool" For Your Detective Bag

Accept Your Duty: Being a _____ means accepting your
_____ as Peter described in 1 Peter 3:15. Recommit yourself as a
Christian to learn about the evidence for Jesus and for God's existence.
Become a Christian _____ .

J. Warner and Susie Wallace

Chapter 3 Note Sheet - Time to Train
Forensic Faith for Kids

Why is Daniel so eager to find Bailey's home?

_____

_____

Why is Hannah eager to investigate what Jesus said about
Himself?

_____

_____

_____

Detective Jeffries draws a diagram on the whiteboard. Fill-in what's missing below then sketch in
the complete diagram on the next image to the right next to Detective Jeffries:

TRAIN
Frustrating

_____

Task

According to Detective Jeffries, why
are frustrating tests important? Why
do they make us better "detectives"?

_____

_____

_____

_____

Detective Jeffries says, "Everything you _____,
study, and learn between the _____ you've
experienced so far and the success I'm sure you'll achieve
will come as the result of _____."

"When someone like Marco says something untrue about
Christianity and you're not sure how to respond, just say,
'That's interesting, let me do some _____ and I'll
get back to you.' Then start _____."

A "Tool" For Your Detective Bag

Enjoy the Tests: Has anyone ever challenged your faith? Don't be afraid
of _____! They are valuable "_____" that can motivate
you to become a better Christian Case Maker. Let each challenge
motivate you to become a good _____.

J. Warner and Susie Wallac[e]

Chapter 5 Note Sheet - Determined to Be Detectives
Forensic Faith for Kids

Why do you, Daniel and Jasmine go to the library?

_____

_____

What is the name of the book you find?

_____

Why do you think this book might be helpful?

_____

_____

What is the name of Hannah's friend who joins them (she's Pastor Woods' daughter)? _____

Pastor Woods opens his bible and places it next to Jason's notepad. "As you take your notes on your _____, don't be afraid to write in your _____."

"It's not against the rules to write in your _____." Says Pastor Woods. "God is pleased when we take His Word _____ and study it."

What does Detective Jeffries say about what you, Daniel and Jasmine learned at the library?

_____

_____

Detective Jeffries tells Jason and Hannah, "I'm very _____ with your efforts. I gave you careful instructions, and I can see you've followed them. I think you're all about to make a big _____."

A "Tool" For Your Detective Bag

Be Thorough, Alert and Detailed: Be sure to take great notes and be alert to anything or everything that will help you solve _____ or make a case. Look for the things that are *hiding in* _____ sight.

J. Warner and Susie Wallace

Chapter 7 Note Sheet - What Should We Say?
Forensic Faith for Kids

Why does chaos break out at Mrs. Stallings' pet shop?

_____

_____

Mrs. Stallings remembers selling Bailey's collar to a woman. How does she describe the lady who bought the collar?

_____

_____

_____

Mrs. Stallings description of Bailey's owner is different than the one offered by Mr. Terry. Hannah says, "_____ don't usually agree about everything. It doesn't mean they are lying - in fact, you should be _____ if the witness do agree about every _____. It's natural for two or three witnesses to describe things slightly _____."

Detective Jeffries says, "Once you've _____ something, it's time to tell others about what you've _____, and good _____ do two things..." Fill-in his whiteboard drawing to the right:

TO BE A GOOD COMMUNICATOR...
1. Know_____you are talking to
2. Teach them the truth about_____

RULES ABOUT EVIDENCE

1. Just because someone writes something in a____, it doesn't mean it's_____

2. _____has the potential to be evidence

3. The more_____the case, the more reasonable the conclusion

Now fill-in the rules Detective Jeffries wrote on the whiteboard (to the left). Detective Jeffries said: "But, after you've taught Marco all of this, I want you to be _____ for something," continues Jeffries. "Even if you do a great job telling Marco the truth about Jesus, he still might not _____ to what you have to say. Remember, he might be just like the author of the book - not everyone is _____ to hear the truth."

A "Tool" For Your Detective Bag

Know and Help Your Listeners: When you share the truth about Jesus with your friends or family members, _____ all you can about them. Then teach them something about how we figure out what is true. Listen carefully, pray often, and help your listeners _____.

J. Warner and Susie Wallac

Once you've completed *Forensic Faith for Kids* and assembled the Fill-In and Activity Sheets in your Academy Notebook, you're ready to graduate!

There are two ways to get your Certificate of Graduation:

Cut out the 5 x 7 Certificate at the back of this book, add your name, and frame it.

or

Visit the ForensicFaithforKids.com website and print the 8 x 10 Certificate (ask your parent for help if you want to download the customizable version). Add your name, and frame it.

Cadet Academy

FORENSIC FAITH

CERTIFICATE OF QUALIFICATION

Has Successfully Completed the Forensic Faith Cadet Academy and Has Therefore Earned This

Adult Supervisor

Training Detective